Instant Wind Forecasting

By the same author

Wind and Sailing Boats
Weather Forecasting Ashore and Afloat
The Wind Pilot
* Instant Weather Forecasting 2nd edition
Basic Windcraft
Cruising Weather
Dinghy and Boardsailing Weather
Reading the Weather: Modern Techniques for Yachtsmen
Sailing off the Beach
* The Weather Handbook

* Published by Sheridan House

Alan Watts

Instant Wind Forecasting

SHERIDAN HOUSE

First published in the United States 2002
by Sheridan House Inc.
145 Palisade Street
Dobbs Ferry, NY 10522
www.sheridanhouse.com

All photographs by the author
except for No 23 which is by Inge Moore

First paperback edition 1988
by Adlard Coles

While all reasonable care has been taken in the publication of this
book, the publisher takes no responsibility for the use of the
methods or products described in the book.

Library of Congress Cataloging-in-Publication Data

Watts, Alan, 1925–
    Instant wind forecasting/Alan Watts
       p.cm
    Originally published: New York: Dodd, Mead, 1975.
    ISBN 1-57409-143-3 (pbk.)
    1. Wind forecasting. I. Title.

    QC931.W3 2002
    551.64'18—dc21   2001034836

Printed in Hong Kong

ISBN 1-57409-143-3

Once, during a long hot summer, I put together the book called *Instant Weather Forecasting*. It was perhaps a dangerous thing to attempt to compartmentalize the weather, but because it is based on well-known meteorological principles many people have found *Instant Weather Forecasting* helpful. This is, I think, mainly due to the fact that the book suggests to people what might happen and then leaves them to make up their own minds as to whether it will indeed do what they expect. The book has been translated into almost all the European languages and has to date sold some half million copies. It has recently been reissued in a Second Edition after being continuously in print for over 40 years.

When I thought about the far more dangerous idea of compart-mentalizing the wind it seemed fairly natural to call the book *Instant Wind Forecasting*. But I know that the wind forecasting you do from this book will very often be far from 'instant'. However, compared with other books on this subject, this book may have pretensions to living up to its name.

I have tried to make it a practical book that people can take with them to supplement and amplify the forecasts they hear and see. Radio and TV forecasts will only give the general trend of the wind's direction and speed; the actual wind may easily be made very different by the terrain or by being near the coast.

Since yacht racing is so wind-intensive, with every shift being of great importance, the book is particularly aimed at dinghy, board and deep keel helmsmen and tacticians. However, it also has something to say to glider and hang-glider pilots, to golfers when the wind is gusting across the fairway, and to ornithologists and entomologists studying the effects of wind on the flight of birds and insects.

Helmsmen of sailing boats cannot expect to get a race-winning idea out of this book every time or even most of the time. What I hope they *will* get is an idea of what to expect and so be ready to meet a windshift when it comes – whenever it comes. For the time

at which a wind may shift is subject to uncertainties that may amount to tens of minutes at best or hours at worst. Yet ten minutes indecision may lose a dinghy race, and an hour can do the same on the ocean. There are *some* big shifts, like sea breeze shifts, over which nature has built telltale clouds, and what these usually look like has been emphasized in the text. In fact very few major wind shifts occur without some sign being evident in the clouds above. The problem for the non-meteorologist it to recognize those signs.

With the photos and cross references to help I hope many situations that are amenable to some kind of wind forecasting have been covered. There are many days when the wind blows from one quarter and stays there. It is the days when wind shifts occur and when the shifts can, in some way, be predicted that have been covered in this book. Only familiarity and use will show you which pages are most useful for a specific situation.

Let me make it clear that *Instant Wind Forecasting* is not a text-book on the wind. There is very little deep explanation here – just enough to make it understandable. It is designed to be a kind of instant guide to winds that may be useful, based on the look of the sky and the feel of the day. This approach may appeal to all those who are daunted by long-winded explanations. Perhaps then, knowing that something may happen, the interested observer will keep a weather eye cocked to the sky to see if he can detect when it will happen. For undoubtedly even today, when so much more is known than in the past, knowledge of the wind is the most neglected part of the spectrum of sea-going knowledge among small craft sailors. Other sportsmen may not even think that there is anything to learn.

This book demands very little in the way of meteorological knowl-edge. Try using it and do not give up even if it does not seem to work very well at first.

Alan Watts
2001

Instant Wind Forecasting is designed to help sort out the probable trends in the wind from a mass of possibilities. The wind you have now may shift or it may remain the same. If it remains the same then sail to that wind, but if it shifts then you have to re-orientate your thoughts and your tactics.

So first use the book to determine the probable trends of the wind and then fine down the details until you think you have a more definite idea of what it will do over the period of your sail, cruise or race. There are, however, so many types of wind and weather and so many different sailing venues that no book, however detailed, could hope to cover them all.

In thinking about the layout I have tried to make the book practical by suggesting what can happen as definitely as possible—and that has not been easy. However, there are some certainties. What will the reader know definitely about the situation? He will know where he intends to be at some future time and usually he is on time or will get there sometime. As the wind tends to be dictated in its local behaviour by the juxtaposition of land and water the information has been divided by zones. Either to seaward of the main coastline or, on some land-locked waters, to landward of it.

What next? The state of the sky and the feel of the day are there to be sampled. You know what the wind and weather are now, or what they are forecast to be for some later time. So the second division is into days that are easily recognizable.

Here the restriction is to days that produce recognizable wind shifts. Every day produces wind shifts, but if there is little or no prospect of divining them in advance then you can only sail to windward on headers and hope for the best. For example, blue skies with heap clouds (Cu) have been specially well covered because they produce a definite shift pattern and when the wind is light enough they positively encourage sea breezes by day. When the cloud dies out overland by night, nocturnal winds are actively promoted. Then there are days that look and

feel thundery and are rather oppressive even if they do not actually produce thunder. On such days the shift pattern is often bold and decisive, even if the wind strength is quite low. And so on.

There will, inevitably, be many days which do not fit the patterns chosen, but by making a choice I have tried to eliminate vagueness. Days whose aspects do not fit one or other of the days described tend to have vague wind patterns that cannot be used to much advantage. Those that are described tend to have shifts that can be considered and utilized.

Then there is the question of doing the greatest good for the greatest number. That means giving most information for the coastal regions where the vast majority go afloat. There *is* information for deep inland and far offshore regions but it is inevitably sparse. It means that the wind that nature designed for the coastal day sailor—the sea breeze—gets a good deal of attention and the nocturnal wind, when dinghy sailors sleep, gets less space. In any case there is less to be said about the nocturnal wind than about the sea breeze. The latter holds sway over thousands of miles of coastal water in the spring and summer months.

So here are the main divisions of the book:

Section A (9–22) **The Strength of the Wind and the Waves**.
General information on the wind and wave heights especially for those going clear of the land.

Section B (24–37) **Wind Shifts of Poor Weather**.
Hints and suggestions on the likely wind shifts when the weather is not very good—or just plain bad.

Section C (38–61) **Local Wind Shifts**.
An important part of the book, as it deals with the shifts with which the majority of sailors have to contend.

Section D (64–73) **Micro-wind Shifts**.
Suggestions on recognition of airstreams and the tactics to adopt in them.

Section E (74–105) **Sailing Days with Recognizable Wind.**
Patterns
   Sailing off the coast or inland from it? This section can be consulted to suggest likely shifts. The landward zones are those of maximum wind shift, both in degree and frequency and since they are habitually frequented by small craft, are of the utmost importance.
Section F (106–13) **Inland Sailing.**
   Shoreside topography and hamper often dictate the wind on inland waters. Included are hints and prompts on what to consider when confronted with an unknown body of inland water.
Section G (116–17) **Winds over the Great Lakes.**
   American and Canadian sailors frequent the greatest extent of inland water in the world. What we learn from the Great Lakes can be applied, with reservations, to similar large bodies of inland water.
   The above sections describe the contents of the book but the reader may still wonder where to find the information he wants.
   A source of general information is **The Wind's Day** (43–5) which will prompt suggestions as to what the wind might do. Then consult the more detailed sections to see if it is actually likely to do it. A couple of examples may help.

Example 1   You are intending to sail a dinghy on a creek or estuary that is within a mile or two of the main coastline (the Beachland zone), you expect to set out in the morning and come back later in the afternoon.
   Unless already familiar with it, consult *The Wind's Day* to remind yourself of what winds might blow. Match your day to one of those in Section E and read the relevant entries. If the weather looks different then experience can help to fit your day to one of the chosen situations.
   Suppose the morning conditions are of mainly blue skies in which Cu clouds may develop later. Consult (90) for the times

of day involved and so obtain more details of the likely wind changes. Then for more specific information consult section C Local Wind Shifts. If you are racing, the micro-wind shifts likely to be encountered can be found on (64) and (68).

Example 2   You are planning to cruise coastwise when the weather is apparently fair, but the forecast warns of troughs of low pressure crossing the area. While still in harbour you can assess the strength of the wind at sea (17) and add the likely gusts (19). You can also assess the likely wave height (20).
   Watch the weather and decide where you are in the weather scene by using the photos to recognize the skies ahead of troughs or fronts (88), e.g. (87) well ahead; (35) ahead; (26) nearer; (23) close to; (27) passing. Passing fronts and troughs mean permanent wind shifts later (30). It might mean a really big blow developing (36). In any case, listen to the forecast and see what it says. If you cannot, then use all the aids this, or any other book, provides to assess the likely trends. If it then appears to be not too bad for you and your crew, then go—and good luck.

Cloud abbreviations

Cumulus	Cu	Altocumulus	Ac
Stratocumulus	Sc	Altostratus	As
Cumulonimbus	Cb	Cirrus	Ci
Stratus	St	Cirrocumulus	Cc
Nimbostratus	Ns	Cirrostratus	Cs

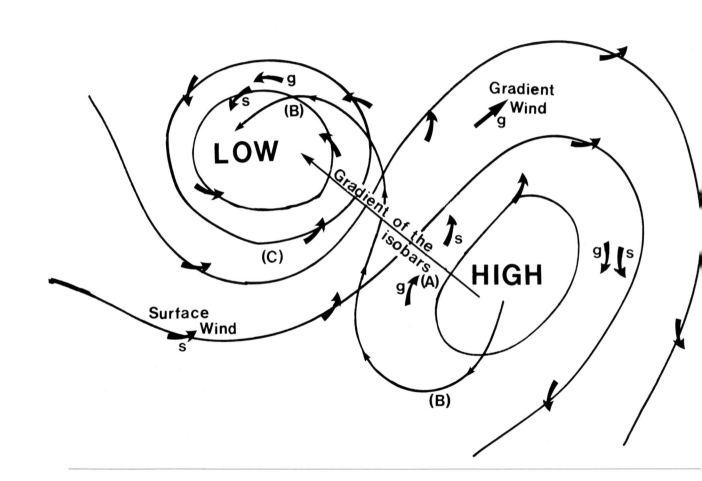

Wind blows from where pressure is high to where it is low, Fig. 1. It does not go directly down the 'gradient' of pressure (A). Because of the rotation of the Earth it spirals out of high pressure regions into low pressure ones (B).

In the Northern Hemisphere:

The wind blows to keep Low pressure on its Left (C).

(In the Southern Hemisphere for Left read Right).

This produces the practical rule:

Stand back to the wind and pressure is Low on your Left.

(In the Southern Hemisphere read 'Stand facing the wind etc.').

These rules apply to the temperate latitudes most strongly. In the tropics the winds tend to move more directly from high to low pressure. This book concerns the temperate latitudes and most of what is said will apply to either hemisphere. It is written for the Northern Hemisphere, but corrections for the Southern Hemisphere are noted where appropriate.

Gradient wind is that wind which blows round pressure systems (arrows marked g). The **isobars** (lines of equal pressure) are akin to contours of height. Thus we speak of the 'gradient' of the isobars. The closer the isobars the 'tighter' the gradient and the stronger the gradient wind. There will be fresh to strong winds at (C) where the isobars are closely spaced but less wind at (A). The gradient wind blows along the direction of the isobars.

Surface wind is the gradient wind that has been modified by friction of the surface (arrows marked s). The greater the friction the more the surface wind differs in speed and direction from the true gradient wind. However, there is rarely more than a 45° difference between surface and gradient wind directions except when local winds blow. Surface wind is angled in towards low pressure and differs from the gradient wind by 10–15° over the sea and 20–30° over the land. While the angle over the sea is usually about the value quoted, that over the land can be larger or smaller than the quoted values (117).

In this book the word 'gradient' is used to describe the surface wind when that wind is due to pressure systems and not to local winds or topography.

Local winds will modify the above rules.

The most important coastal winds are sea breezes by day and nocturnal winds by night.

The **wind regime of a coast** is governed by the pressure gradient wind and modified by

a. the diurnal variation in wind speed.

b. the sea breeze–nocturnal wind system.

Diurnal variation means the normal change that occurs at almost all land stations through 24 hours. This is covered in table form (44) (*The Wind's Day*). There is also some diurnal variation over the deep ocean and in winds with a long sea fetch, but it is small compared to that over land or in winds with a long land fetch.

The **sea breeze–nocturnal wind** system is one where the winds swing off the sea during the day and off the land during the night. Such a simple statement covers a multitude of variations some of which are covered in the tables.

Other local coastal winds are:

Coastal slope winds due to cold air cascading down steep mountain slopes that come close to the sea. (The Mistral and Bora of the Mediterranean are examples.)

Downdraught winds that accompany thunderstorms and heavy showers especially when these occur on coastal slopes.

Katabatic winds that blow downhill, especially at night in settled weather.

Anabatic winds that lift up hillsides that catch the morning sun.

Mountain and valley winds that blow up the valleys by day and down them at night.

Coastal slope and downdraught winds may accompany poor weather, but katabatics and anabatics, sea breezes and land breezes, and mountain and valley winds are mainly phenomena of settled weather.

How to Judge Wind Speed

Judging wind speed is difficult. It depends on where you are when you attempt to make an estimate. Hints on this are given on the next page and also on (17). The estimated speed is assumed to be the mean speed. On to that you have to add the gusts, (19)
Once the preserve of the professional meteorologist, the masthead anemometer is almost a standard fitting these days for cruising and

The Scale of Wind Speed

Admiral Beaufort's Scale of Wind Speed was fine for men-of-the-line, but needs modifying for small craft use.

Beaufort number	General description	Limit of mean speed (knots)	Land signs	Dinghy criteria
0	Calm	less than 1	Smoke rises vertically. Leaves do not stir	Sails will not fill. Racing flag will not respond. Flies and tell tails might just respond
1	Light air	1 to 3	Smoke drifts. Wind vanes do not respond	Sails fill. Racing flag may not be reliable. Flies and tell tails respond. Crew and helmsman on opposite sides of craft
2	Light breeze	4 to 6	Wind felt on the face. Leaves rustle. Light flags not extended. Wind vanes respond	Useful way can be made. Racing flag reliable. Helmsman and crew both sit to windward. Spinnakers may fill
3	Gentle breeze	7 to 10	Light flags extended. Leaves in constant motion	Helmsman and crew sit on weather gunwale. Spinnakers fill. Fourteen-footers and above may plane
4	Moderate breeze	11 to 16	Most flags extend fully. Small branches move. Dust and loose paper may be raised	Dinghy crews lie out. Twelve-foot dinghies may plane; longer dinghies will plane. The best general working breeze
5	Fresh breeze	17 to 21	Small trees in leaf sway. Tops of tall trees in noticeable motion	Dinghies ease sheets in gusts. Crews use all weight to keep craft upright. Genoas near their limit. Some capsizes
6	Strong breeze	22 to 27	Large branches in motion. Whistling heard in wires	Dinghies overpowered when carrying full sail. Many capsizes. Crews find difficulty in holding craft upright even when spilling wind

racing craft. These instruments are calibrated in knots. A dinghy helmsman will not have such a device, so his criteria are based on observation of the extension of flags etc. and a force is all that he can expect to estimate. Dinghy crews will often be able to read a clubhouse anemometer before they go out, but will have to add extra wind speed to compensate for clearing the land.

Deep keel criteria	State of sea (see (20) for details)	Local wind criteria near shore and on landlocked or inland water
Boom swings idly in the swell. Racing flags and anemometers will not respond. Flies and tell tails might just	Sea mirror-smooth. Calm enough to preserve shape of reflections of sails, masts etc.	Local wind-making forces totally dominant. Seek shores for thermals
Sails just fill, but little way made. Racing flags and vanes may respond but cup anemometers may not. Flies and tell tails respond. Spinnakers do not fill	Scaly or shell-shaped ripples. No foam crests to be seen on open sea	Local winds still dominant. Sea breezes will set in in forenoon. Nocturnal winds at night. The wind may already be a local one. On lakes, rivers etc. anabatic or katabatic winds
Wind felt on the cheek. Controlled way made. Spinnakers and sails generally fill. Racing flags and anemometers respond and are reliable	Small short wavelets with glassy crests that do not break	Local winds can easily influence this wind speed. Sea breezes set in by midday. Usual upper limit to nocturnal winds. Mountain and valley winds achieve this speed and more
Good way made. Light flags fully extended	Large wavelets. Crests may break but foam is of glassy appearance. A few scattered white horses may be seen when wind at upper limit	Sea breezes set in against this speed but usually not until afternoon. Allow earlier time in southern latitudes. Nocturnal winds do not often modify a gradient that is blowing at this speed in evening and early night
Best general working breeze for all craft. Genoas at optimum	Small waves lengthen. Fairly frequent white horses	Stronger local winds influence this speed. Sea breezes may set in in late afternoon. Too strong normally for nocturnal winds to modify greatly. However, allow for effects of high ground near the shore
Craft's way somewhat impeded by seaway. Genoas near their limit. Spinnakers still carried. Yachts approach maximum speed	Moderate waves. Many white horses	Upper limit to winds that can be modified by local influences except in southern latitudes. Sea breeze effects only serve to shift the direction of winds of this strength— if at all
Edge of 'yacht gale' force. Cruising craft seek shelter. Reefing recommended to meet gusts when cruising	Large waves form and extensive foam crests are prevalent. Spray may be blown off some wave tops	Not normally influenced by local wind effects

11

(Contd. over)

The Scale of Wind Speed (Contd.)

Beaufort number	General description	Limit of mean speed (knots)	Land signs	Dinghy criteria
7	Near gale (American usage: Moderate gale)	28 to 33	Whole trees in motion. Inconvenience felt when walking against wind	Dinghies fully reefed. Difficult to sail even o main alone. This is the absolute top limit for dinghies—other than *in extremis*
8	Gale (Fresh gale)	34 to 40	Twigs broken off trees. Generally impeded progress on foot. Rarely experienced inland	Dinghies may survive if expertly handled in the seaway on foresail alone
9	Severe gale (Strong gale)	41 to 47	Chimney pots and slates removed. Fences blown down etc.	Not applicable
10	Storm (Whole gale)	48 to 55	Very rare inland. Trees uprooted; considerable structural damage	Not applicable

Deep keel criteria	State of sea (See (20) for details)	Local wind criteria near shore and on landlocked or inland water
Yacht gale force when most cruising craft seek shelter. Racing yachts may just carry spinnakers. Reefing essential	Sea heaps up and white foam from breaking waves begins to be blown in streaks along the wind direction	Not applicable
Gale force in anybody's language. Only necessity or ocean racing keeps craft at sea. Set storm canvas or heave-to	Moderately high waves of greater length. Edges of crests begin to break into spindrift. Foam blown in well-marked streaks along the wind	Not applicable
Unless ocean racing—and sometimes even then—craft seek deep water. Run towing warps etc. This may be survival force for most	High waves. Dense streaks of foam along the wind. Crests begin to topple, tumble and roll over	Not applicable
Almost the ultimate for yachts. Only chance in deep water and with sea room to run before it or possibly lie to a sea anchor	Very high waves with long overhanging crests. The whole surface of the sea takes on a white appearance. Tumbling of sea heavy and shocklike. Visibility impaired	Not applicable

13

How to Obtain a Reliable Wind Assessment

Photo 1 *(p. 14)*
Before the race you have time to look at flags and anemometers. But when the shore is crowded by buildings and trees the only true wind direction comes from observing the direction of the Cu clouds above. They give the 'gradient wind' direction. The surface wind will be backed (shifted anticlockwise) from this and altered by shoreside hamper.

In the following pages an assessment of what the wind will do is based on knowing how it is behaving at present. Here are some tips for obtaining a reliable wind speed and direction.

1. The most reliable mean wind speed and direction comes from an anemograph (a chart of the variations). The local weather station probably has one, so telephone them and ask for the mean wind speed and direction and the average gust speed. At the same time you can ask if any major changes are expected.

2. Failing that, use the anemometer on the clubhouse or the masthead anemometer on a yacht at anchor, or tied up in a nearby marina. It is useless looking at the dials for a couple of seconds and deciding that what they show is the wind speed you require. Normally you will not get a reliable mean wind in less than 3–4 minutes observation due to gust cells and turbulence. On days of abnormal variability (72) you ought to note the speed and direction every half minute or so over a period of 15 minutes. If that is too much trouble, then be content not to know the wind direction to better than within 20–30° of its mean value. If it is showery, the most reliable guide to the mean wind is the wind speed obtained when the skies are mainly blue between the showers.

3. If you have no anemometer, you can observe the racing flags on beached dinghies in the open or the race pennants on a starting-box mast. While ashore look into the eye of the wind and see if there is a free run for the wind. If so, accept that the observed speed and direction are the correct ones over the land. Speed will have to be assessed in the open using the Scale of Wind Speed (10–13).

Are you Clear of Obstructions to the Wind?

If an upwind barrier of trees, buildings etc. is apparently the same height as your thumbnail held upright at arm's length, you are outside the wind shadow of the barrier. As you approach it, the effect of the barrier progressively cuts the wind speed until the barrier fits the distance from thumb-tip to first finger-tip of the outstretched hand held at arm's length. At this distance off you may have as little as a fifth of the speed in the open.

Closer to trees you have 20 per cent more than at the previous distance, but with solid buildings etc. you have practically no speed at all.

Concerning the Mean Wind

For sailing dinghies the mean wind has a speed and direction you meet very rarely, compared to speeds and directions that are different from the mean. This text cannot concern itself with the niceties of how meteorologists record the wind using anemographs (chart-drawing anemometers). Most of what you might like to know about such things is in *Wind and Sailing Boats* but here, where the author is very conscious of the title of this book, all that can be said is that the wind spends most of its time shifting backwards and forwards about the so-called 'mean' direction, and all its time rising above and falling below the mean speed. No other sport is so dependent on the 'right-now' wind as dinghy sailing. We shall try to help distinguish between those days when the wind is very variable about its mean direction (64–73) and when it is not. Once you have recognize that the airstream is variable, you sail on the instant wind and make your tactical moves as far as possible in accordance with the ideas given on those pages. If not, you adopt the age-old dictum when sailing to windward—tack when headed by the wind. It's a pretty chancy business and often you are induced to tack by an ephemeral shift that hurries by and leaves you far worse off than before. Such is the sailing life.

How Strong is the Wind at Sea?

Photo 2 *(p. 15)*
Crews who sail from the beach to the open sea must allow for the wind that blows off the land becoming considerably stronger once it breaks clear of the land hamper. The same goes for all who leave harbour for the open sea and beginners who leave the shelter of the clubhouse for more open waters.

Most weather stations are ashore so the wind speed given to you as the actual speed when you contact a weather station is the speed over the land. This is always less than the wind at sea. It may be less by a factor as big as 5, although such a difference is rare and only occurs with light winds. The most likely wind speed at sea, both by day and by night, is given in this table, assuming that you get an actual wind speed from a coastal weather station (one within 2–4 miles (3–7 km) of the coastline).

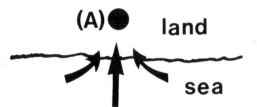

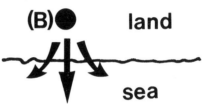

Winds from the Sea				Winds from the Land			
Wind speed quoted by shore station (A)		Wind at sea in knots (Force)		Wind speed quoted by shore station (B)		Wind at sea in knots (Force)	
knots	(Force)	by day	by night	knots	(Force)	by day	by night
0–10	(0–3)	1–14 (1–4)	1–18 (1–5)	0–3	(0–1)	1–10 (1–3)	0–12 (1–4)
11–16	(4)	12–18 (4–5)	19–27 (5–6)	4–6	(2)	10–16 (4)	12–18 (4–5)
17–21	(5)	22–27 (6)	27–33 (7)	7–10	(3)	14–20 (4–5)	15–22 (5)
22–27	(6)	31–38 (7–8)	34–42 (8–9)	11–16	(4)	17–22 (5)	17–26 (5–6)
28–32	(7)	36–42 (8–9)	45–50 (9–10)	17–21	(5)	23–30 (6–7)	26–33 (7)
				22–27	(6)	30–38 (7–8)	33–42 (8)
				28–33	(7)	38–46 (8–9)	40–50 (9–10)

Notes. When winds are from the sea, coastal stations record speeds closer to those at sea—especially by day. The greatest differences between land and sea speeds occur when winds are blowing from the land at night. The above speeds refer to a standard height of about 33 ft (10 metres) which is nicely close to sailplan height. If a station is exposed on the coast and about 150 ft (45 m) above the sea the speeds it quotes as actuals must be dropped by a factor of 25 per cent.

How Strong are the Gusts?

Photo 3 *(opposite)*
Narrow waters and a fresh Cu airstream produce the conditions for maximum difference in speed between gusts and lulls. Shore hamper cuts the lulls while Cu clouds indicate gusts that suddenly come down over the trees. The time is late morning. Someone (centre) has already succumbed to the stab of a rogue gust.

Gusts are faster wind from aloft brought down to the surface. They are not impeded by surface obstacles unless you are very close to those obstacles. **Lulls** are surface wind that is impeded by surface obstacles.
   The difference between mean wind speed and the speed of the gusts is greater when
1. sailing on land-locked waters
2. heap clouds (Cu and Cb) clouds are about
3. sailing in the morning rather than the afternoon
4. the speed is about Force 5 (17–21 kt). The difference is smaller for lesser and stronger winds.
   The difference is less when
5. one is at sea and clear of the land
6. conditions are meteorologically stable, i.e. layer clouds (and no heap clouds) with poor visibility, compared to the excellent visibility enjoyed with a Cu airstream
7. sailing at night (which includes the evening and the period around dawn).
Gusts make the wind strength experienced by the yacht feel stronger, for it is the recurrent gusts that have to be fought and overcome. So we define a **mean gust speed** which is the strongest wind that regularly occurs, and a **maximum gust speed** which will occur occasionally in any run of the wind. Figures for both of these can be given taking into account the above factors (1) to (4).

Mean wind speed as measured or forecast	6–10 kt Force 3	11–16 kt Force 4	17–21 kt Force 5	22–27 kt Force 6	28–33 kt Force 7	34–48 kt Force 8–9
Mean gust speed to expect	Force 4	Force 5	Force 6–7	Force 7–8	40–47 kt Force 9	48–57 kt Force 10
Maximum gust speed to expect	Force 5	Force 6	Force 7	Force 9	Force 9–10	Force 11

Gustiness at sea (when the wind has a sea fetch of over 50 miles) does not differ much between day and night and therefore, as gusts are difficult to detect at night, allow only sufficient sail to comfortably contain the maximum gust speed.
Thunderstorms produce very intense gusts that follow some pre-storm wind regime. Because of the way storms are constructed we can give some guidance as follows:
Wind regime before storm:
Wind away from or across path of the storm (not usually above 20 kt)   Expect gusts of 25–35 kt
Wind towards storm (not usually above 10 kt)   Expect gusts of 30–50 kt
Really bad storms can produce 60 knots or more at their leading edges.
A curious attribute of thundery situations is that storms a hundred miles away may induce gusts in an otherwise benign airstream. The most likely time for this is at night. The gusts may not exceed 25–30 kt, but when the average wind is 5–10 kt that is a dangerous increase. (see *Wind and Sailing Boats*, 165).

19

Wave height depends on
1. wind strength
2. duration. The time that the wind has blown within 30° of a given direction.
3. fetch. The distance wind can run from the nearest sizeable land mass.

Coastal waters (depths of 150 ft or less)

Fetch (nautical miles)	5	10	20	50	100	200	500
Force 3 (7–10 kt)							
Wave height in feet	—	1	2	3	3	4	4
Duration (hours)	—	3	5	10	18	24	48
Force 4 (11–16 kt)							
Height	1	2	3	5	6	7	7
Duration	$1\frac{1}{2}$	2	4	6	12	24	48
Force 5 (17–21 kt)							
Height	2	3	5	8	10	11	12
Duration	1	2	3	6	11	22	48
Force 6 (22–27 kt)							
Height	2–3	4	7	11	14	15	16
Duration	1	2	3	5	10	18	48
Force 7 (28–33 kt)							
Height	3–4	6	10	16	20	22	24
Duration	1	$1\frac{1}{2}$	2	5	8	18	48
Force 8 (34–40 kt)							
Height	4–5	8	14	22	27	28	30
Duration	1	$1\frac{1}{2}$	2	4	7	15	36
Force 9 (41–48 kt)							
Height	6	10	18	28	35	38	40
Duration	1	1	2	4	6	12	26

Oceanic Waters (more than 600 ft deep)

Fetch (nautical miles)	5	10	20	50	100	200	500
Force 3 (7–10 kt)							
Wave height in feet	—	—	1	2	2	2	2
Duration in hours	—	—	4	7	13	24	48
Force 4 (11–16 kt)							
Height	—	1	2	3	4	4	4
Duration	—	2	3	6	12	22	48
Force 5 (17–21 kt)							
Height	1	2	4	6	8	8	8
Duration	1	2	3	5	11	18	48
Force 6 (22–27 kt)							
Height	3	4	7	10	13	14	14
Duration	1	2	3	5	10	18	36
Force 7 (28–33 kt)							
Height	4	6	10	16	19	20	21
Duration	1	2	2	4	8	12	30
Force 8 (34–40 kt)							
Height	5	8	14	23	27	29	30
Duration	1	1	2	4	6	12	30
Force 9 (41–47 kt)							
Height	8	12	20	33	40	42	44
Duration	1	1	2	3	6	10	24
Force 10 (48–55 kt)							
Height	9	14	27	45	52	56	60
Duration	1	1	2	3	5	10	24

(The figures are based on graphs appearing with 'Forecasting Wind-generated Sea Waves'. Darbyshire and Draper, *Engineering*, 5 April 1963.)

How High are the Waves at Sea? (Contd.)

Most probable maximum wave height in storm

Duration	1	3	6	12	18	24	36
Multiply figures on previous page by	1.18	1.28	1.33	1.4	1.42	1.45	1.47

Example   The wind is estimated to have blown at about Force 6 for 4 hours from a direction where the land mass is 100 miles away. What should the wave height be? *Answer:* 14 ft from the table, but it takes 11 hours to develop this height so the waves will not be 14 ft yet. In practice, interpolation between height for 4 hours duration at this speed, whatever the fetch (in this case 8 ft) will give a reliable estimate.

Photo 4 *(opposite)*
The biggest seas usually come with cyclonic weather of long duration. The sky here is typical of cyclonic weather and is almost permanently cloudy. There are occasional breaks but they are short lived. However, strong winds on the edges of anticyclones also build up the sea under broken or even clear skies on some occasions. Treat the cloud line in the middle with respect, it may mean a sudden wind increase or shift.

WIND SHIFTS OF POOR WEATHER: Cyclonic Winds

Photo 5 *(p. 26)*
A typical sky ahead of gathering bad weather. These are the clouds brought in ahead of warm fronts or occlusions. There is thin, featureless, As cloud above the dying remains of Cu that populated the recent fair weather. Soon the Cu will be gone and the sky will be totally grey and flat. Rain will come when low cloud again forms under the cloudbase and with it, very often, stronger wind.

Main recognition points: much cloudiness with periods of rain, drizzle or showers, mixed with more continuous rain. The general tendency of weather conditions is to deteriorate. Breaks occur to reveal much upper cloud, only to close in again with low overcast. Winds are cool and 'heavy' with moisture. Troughs of low pressure rotate about an almost stationary low centre and bring a continuous succession of frontal situations. In summer heavy thunderstorms may be induced in the circulation. The poor cyclonic weather may persist for days, only gradually tending to improve. Visibility can often be poor—amounting to fog when cloud is low and when rain or drizzle falls.

Surface direction	Wind was	Low centre should	Wind shift in next few hours should	Weather now should be	Expect
East (often not above moderate strength, can be quite light)	More S and has backed E	Lie to SW of position and should track to S of position	Remain E or back farther to NE. Some increase in speed	Deteriorating from fair with increasing high cloud (possibly as in photo 6). High or medium level cloud moving in from S. If likely to be thundery then sky like (71) or (103)	More cloud. Lower base. Rain or drizzle. If base does not become low then centre probably moving 100 to 200 miles south of position
South-east (Not often above moderate and sometimes lighter)	W or SW earlier, now backed round to SE	Lie to W and probably track across position or to N of position	Remain SE or veer slightly S if wind gets up	Increasing high cloud perhaps as photo 6 or (103). If like (35) then see (36). High cloud should move in from SW or W. See above for thundery lows	Increasing cloud of warm front or occlusion type (26). Rain and low cloud
Southerly	Possibly W or SW now backed to S	Lie to NW and track to N of position	Remain S possibly go SSE—even as far as SE before veering later	As above. High cloud should move in from W or NW	As above
South-west to west	NW or W	Lie to N of position and track some distance from position	Be frontal shifts (i.e. veers) at cold fronts or an occlusion. New direction probably W to NW	Cyclonic type but relatively warm with poor visibility and low cloud. If low cloud broken then much high or medium level cloud often in islands about the sky. Such higher cloud should move from around SW or W	Change to more polar air with Cu or Cb (shower) cloud. However, sometimes this phase is slow to arrive

Forecast or actual weather: centre of low pressure lies close enough to the sailing area for the latter to be fully under the dominance of the low.
Winds: when forecast as 'cyclonic' will vary in the way theory and observation have shown they do when a low centre passes close across you. We can expect the following changes, usually depending on the wind direction ahead of the encroaching depression. The text-book depression is not very prevalent in summer. Winds will rarely advance to full gale and most cyclonic weather will come with winds of Force 4 or less.

Barometer	Consider later	Remarks
Has probably been falling, but not steeply. If steep fall then low probably going to track across you. In this case expect wind increase—even temporary gale	Cyclonic shifts, i.e. backing to N or NW in rear of departing low centre. Improving slowly to fairer, cool conditions. Increasing visibility	The lows considered can be steered by waterways along their lengths, e.g. as occurs along the English Channel. Most lows tend to move from W to E. They can move 'retrograde' when caught in the massive circulation of vast 'blocking' anticyclones. If such odd movement occurs wind sequence is likely to be E–NE or N–E or SE. If low centre tracks directly across position then typical sequence is SE—temporary calm or light variable—picking up from a westerly point
Falling moderately (about 1–2 mb per hour). If steep fall (about 3 mb per hour) indicates developing depression and up to gale force winds (1 mb = 0·03 in. mercury)	Cyclonic shifts. Veering on passage of fronts or troughs to SW or W and eventually NW as low centre clears away	This direction is the typical one ahead of depressions that are passing to the north of the sailing area. It is common over much of the US and Europe
As above	As above	This direction is also a typical one found ahead of temperate latitude lows
Probably has been falling but is now steadier. If still falling expect very poor weather for a time	Fairer conditions after clearance of fronts and the following showers (if any). In this later phase expect sky like (67) or (78)	On a maritime seaboard the SW wind is wet and humid. It produces much cloud. On a continental seaboard the SW wind can be warm and dry but also at times has the warmth and humidity of southern seas

25

(Contd. pp. 28, 29)

Surface direction	Wind was	Low centre should	Wind shift in next few hours should	Weather now should be	Expect
West to north-west	SW	Have passed away to E	Be frontal shifts from W to NW or even N. However, these may have already passed. Then shifts come with showery troughs (95). If still low cloud and rain then expect clearance and veering wind	Rain and showers for a while as the cold front clears—then sky opening up to high cloud and Cu (low) cloud. If front has cleared then weather now is probably clear and cool with Cu or Cb clouds. High cloud behind a clearing cold front should move from SW for real improvement (27)	If wind remains W as fronts and troughs pass, the change to cool polar air will be delayed. If sharp veering shift occurs as front passes, expect cool air and showers. If latter phase is already in being expect slow relaxation to fair conditions (54) or (18)
North to north-east (the latter is an unusual direction to be associated with lows)	1. W–NW	Be to the SE having tracked from N or NE of position	Show little change, but can increase to fresh or more for considerable periods of time	Bright skies and big showers (95). No great change when high cloud tracks from N. If tracks from E then expect slow deterioration, to low cloud and rain or drizzle	Slow change from showery to fair
	2. SE–E	Have been to the S and now be tracking NE away from position	Continue to shift cyclonically (back in this case) as centre tracks past. No great increase in wind speed on most occasions	Overcast with periods of rain or drizzle (23)	Only slow clear-up to brighter conditions, say next day

Photo 6 *(p. 27)*
In a run of cyclonic weather a major trough passes. This is the rear end of a cold front and the wind is strong from right to left. The windshift (a veer) would have come possibly an hour or more before the cloud broke so positively. Showers must be expected to follow and they can be heavy.

Barometer	Consider later	Remarks
Has been lower than now. Should show a rise, but not too fast. If rises very sharply then expect strong wind later—and perhaps not many hours later	Fairer conditions with good visibility cessation of any showers, lightening, possibly backing, winds	A ridge of high pressure, sometimes only of a day's duration, frequently follows the passage of a low. Backing wind is often an early sign of the next depression coming in. The barometer climbing steadily is a good indicator of a ridge that may last a few days—or sometimes a few weeks
Probably shows little change. A slow rise must ensue for the change to fair conditions	Wind to stay in this quarter if a sizeable anticyclone grows to W. Wind will back as a weak ridge passes. Then expect another low	The low producing N or NE winds is often almost stationary in the vicinity. Weather therefore will depend on time and place
Falling somewhat at first, but then slow rise as low passes away	Rather indeterminate conditions to follow. However, any showers should not be heavy. There can be thunder with this sort of low on this kind of track	

Will There be a Permanent Wind Shift?

Winds that shift from one direction to another and stay there for many hours (half a day or a day, or longer for instance) are what is meant by permanent. Permanent shifts occur 1. Slowly and more or less continuously when they are due to shifting pressure patterns. 2. Rapidly and usually once and for all when they are due to passing fronts.

Type of shift	Usual cause	Weather before onset of shift	Signs closer to the shift	Later signs
Slow backing	Approaching trough of low pressure	Fair with very little high cloud. Often Cu clouds. Typical skies (14), (67), (94)	Ci above the lower cloud (54) or encroaching cloud above and on windward horizon (115). Barometer that may have been rising now steadied or falling. Often very good visibility	Increasing high cloud (35). Later—veil of high cloud above dying lower cloud (24). Barometer should now be falling and a westerly is bound to back towards S
Frontal veer (possibly sharp)	Passage of a warm front	Warm front: low cloud, continuous rain, moderate visibility. Previously deteriorated in the normal way with warm fronts (88)	Lowest cloudbase. Steady rain in most cases. Barometer that has been falling may show slight signs of arresting its fall. Scan windward horizon for a line of change akin to (23)	Immediate sign is passing trailing wisps of cloud almost on the deck. Lightening sky behind the murk. Odd crossing motions of lowest visible cloud layers
Frontal veer (probably sharp)	Passage of a cold front	Cold front: warm sector weather with much cloud, at all levels. High humidity. Poor visibility, even fog	Unusual for no form of break in warm sector low cloud before an active cold front clears across. However, sudden showers mixed with rain makes cold front suspect. Barometer may have been steady or falling somewhat after a steady period	Immediate signs: Darker cloudline across the wind. Trailing low cloud moving in from windward. Visible signs of clouds moving in contrasting directions. Sudden showers and rain. Change of cloudbase to higher, perhaps harder immediately behind frontal edge
Frontal veer (normally not sharp)	Passage of an occluded front	Same signs as for a warm front approaching. However, as occlusions are formed late in the history of a low there can be holes in the cloud sheet	Same as for warm front but rain need not be as prolonged nor as continuous as with a true warm front. There is no warm air phase and so rain of warm front changes to showers of cold front without any lengthy cessation between. Moderate pressure fall	As for warm front and cold front combined, but effects are not so marked. Pressure steadies off at front and then rises

Use this page to anticipate coming shifts of wind that are due to pressure systems and fronts. It is mainly for yachtsmen at sea, but can be useful also to small water helmsmen. The shifts will be clockwise (veers) when they occur across fronts and they will almost invariably be anticlockwise (backs) ahead of fronts, troughs and occlusions. In S. Hemisphere for 'veer' read 'back' and vice versa.

Most likely wind regime before shift	Tactical hints	Remarks
W or NW light to moderate. Possibly fresh at sea. For other less likely directions see previous page	If beating into a backing wind pattern stay on port tack as far as possible. If reaching on port you will eventually run before a stronger wind. If reaching on starboard you will eventually be beating. If running then choose port tack if possible	The most prevalent backing shift that lasts for hours is that ahead of approaching troughs of low pressure. The wind will have to veer later however and such veers come at the passage of fronts
SE to S. Moderate to fresh. Possibly gale	The veer to come is preceded by the backing phase, so follow above before shift. Beating on port into a veering shift heads you so choose starboard before the shift and be prepared to round up if the shift is sudden	The shift at a warm front is not often as marked or as sharp as at a cold front—however, as with all things meteorological you cannot be too dogmatic about it
SW moderate to fresh, can be gale. The more virile the whole weather regime the more virile the front and the shift that comes with it	Take port tack ahead of the front itself. Then if possible take starboard tack to avoid being put in irons should the veer be sudden and sharp as it can be. Allow for the truly active front to produce a shift of as much as 90° or more. Shift is under the leading lowest cloud edge, in sharp cases. Many cold fronts are of multiple structure and each mini-front produces part of the final veer. Less active fronts may take an hour or more to produce the final phase of the shift	The cold front has to follow the warm sector air at some time as the weather has to go back to cool polar air. However, allow for the anticyclonic situations where the warm air arrives and no cold air comes for days afterwards. This means using the forecasts as well as observation. The exact moment of wind shift under an active cold front can only be divined by on-the-spot observation
More difficult to assess than for the warm front but usually around S. Wind speed can be moderate or even less when the occlusion is old	Tactics are like those for cold front but expect the whole shifting phase to occupy a relatively long time—possibly an hour or two	As there is no warm sector phase, the shift at an occlusion is like a rather extended form of the cold front. Occlusions that form in the centres of depressions are far more likely to produce intense shifts than ones that have lost much cohesion with the low with which they formed

(Contd. over)

Will there be a Permanent Wind Shift? (Contd.)

Type of shift	Usual cause	Weather before onset of shift	Signs closer to the shift	Later signs
Frontal veer (often weak and sometimes not greatly evident)	Passage of an old, weak, warm front or occlusion	Occluded front: as for warm front	Build-up of cloud sheets of types seen ahead of more virile warm fronts, i.e. Ci (87). Ac and As (103) but light rain or drizzle need only fall from extensive Sc (66). Barometer falls slowly and possibly erratically	Again, judged on the weaker regime, the shift comes where the low cloud sheet breaks to open skies. Sometimes instead of the more normal hard base of Sc there will be some formless low cloud (23) as the shift comes
Frontal veer (often weak and sometimes not greatly evident)	Passage of an old, weak, cold front or occlusion	Cold front: cloud bank arrives overhead, rain and showers but not intense. Possibly only bank of Sc with banks of Ac/As above (63). Some fall in barometer but not marked	Warm air conditions with islands of high cloud. Some low cloud, possibly sea fog but poor visibility in any case. Darker, deeper, cloud line on horizon obviously advancing. Sight of Cb tops (heads like cauliflowers sticking through the lower cloud banks)	The shift will be found to start under the cloud line and continue for a time. There should be a change to Cu clouds and clearer air. Cooler

Note. For permanent wind shifts due to sea breezes (forenoon and afternoon only) see (53) and for those due to nocturnal winds (evening and early night) (58).

Most likely wind regime before shift	Tactical hints	Remarks
Can be any one of many different directions, for these fronts are sometimes drawn into anticyclones. Wind, however, will not usually be strong and may be less than 10 knots	Almost invariably any form of front will produce a back ahead and a veer behind it. So tactical advice must follow that for the virile warm front, but the shift may not be at all marked (10–20° say)	The old front (called a kata-front because the air aloft over it is sinking) is very prevalent over continental areas well removed from the breeding grounds for lows. Eastern Britain and Continental Europe are subject to Atlantic lows and central eastern States to lows born in Alberta etc. However, old fronts can be found mixed up with many extensive anticyclones. Thundery warm fronts (86) must be allowed for in summer
Above remarks apply but the weak cold front is more likely to obey the rules for cold fronts than is an old occlusion	Above remarks apply and advice can be a modified form of that for the active cold front	Above remarks apply. The cold front is likely to become thundery in summer and so rejuvenate itself into a potentially dangerous weather system

Photo 7 *(opposite)*
This is the classic sky some hours ahead of strong to gale force winds. Recognition points are high cloud (Ci) stretched in parallel lines, or banners, across the sky. Perspective makes them appear to converge on the horizon. Cu clouds below stream across in a wind that must come from left of the upper wind (in which the Ci rides) if real deterioration is to ensue. (From the right in Southern Hemisphere.)

Very rapid increase (less than three hours) in the wind to Force 6–7 (25–30 kt) from Force 3–4 (10–15 kt) is rare following a run of fair weather. The big gales of the summer half of the year take as much as 24 hours to develop. Lesser 'yacht gales' usually take between 6 and 10 hours. In any case anticyclonic (fair) weather has to deteriorate. This is the first case considered below. Sky sequence (87), (35), (26), (23), (27).

On the other hand, when the weather is already bad, or has been bad and there is a respite, the wind can increase to danger levels in a much shorter time. A secondary depression is usually to blame.

Type of weather at present	Previous history	First signs 24–12 hrs ahead of Force 6	Later signs 18–6 hrs ahead
1. Anticyclonic. Typically half cover of Cu. Moderate to good visibility. Sea slight to moderate (35) or (54)	A run of cyclonic weather, of which this spell is a respite, e.g. the weather was poor yesterday or the day before and it has now improved *or* A run of fair weather which now shows signs of breaking down, e.g. sunny, light wind the day before yesterday, some high cloud yesterday, increasing cloud today. Possibly thundery tendency	High Ci cloud, typically moving from NW quadrant. These clouds forming into long, teased-out banners resembling the tail of a flying white mare (35). Often no sign in the wind nor in the barometer at this early time when a large vigorous low is coming. Aircraft make dense persistent vapour trails	Increasing high cloud. Milky veil of Cs cloud (26) giving haloes about sun or moon. Wind backing from typically W towards S. Barometer shows steady fall over last few hours. Obvious motion in the Ci that is passing overhead, or has passed, denotes strong wind later. In N Hemisphere (temperate latitudes) high cloud (Ci) must advance from left of surface wind for significant deterioration. In S Hemisphere it must advance from right
2. Cool, showery, cyclonic with a seaway and much heap cloud	Recent passage of a front or trough, i.e. rain and/or showers in a belt that has passed on. Barometer has been low, is now rising (27)	If weather is to improve behind a retreating depression, weather should be showery and remain so for a day or two (79), (95). Suspect another blow if showers, occurring now, die out rapidly with time	Rapid rise in the barometer. Rapid drop in previously high wind speed (say Force 6–8 to Force 3–4 now). Some layer clouds in upper sky. If showery weather to persist then there should not be much upper layer cloud

Thirdly, on the edges of an anticyclone that has persisted for some time and refuses to give way, the wind can grow to gale force as a depression encroaches on it. Winds can then be gale force under fair skies. The weather does not in any way look like (23) or (103) but more like (54) or (78).

Have You Listened To or Looked At the Forecast?

Note. The signs are for normal temperate latitude cyclones and not tropical cyclones.

Short range signs 8–2 hrs ahead	Immediate signs 4–1 hrs ahead	Remarks
Wind very definitely backing into the S. Barometer falling at increasing rate. Sun disappearing into gathering grey cloud layers. Build-up of cloud should be steady without major breaks in the sequence. Long period swell running in from a quarter between direction of high cloud movement and surface wind	Wind speed picking up to fresh. Backing phase steadying off. Low cloud beginning to form under higher grey sheet cloud (26). Possibly some rain. Barometer falling rapidly. If more than 8–10 mb (0.2–0.3 in.) in last 3 hours then gale confidently anticipated. Expect marked wind increase with onset of rain. Look for approaching cloud line that looks low and solid. Wind often comes with that line like (23)	When fair weather is going to deteriorate· then it does so fairly slowly after a run of anticyclonic weather. It does so moderately rapidly when it comes after a short anticyclonic spell between passing lows. It does so rapidly and sometimes without much warning immediately behind a passing depression when the barometer has tended to rise sharply. 'First rise after low foretells a stronger blow' (see section below)
Wind backing rapidly. Barometer steadying off or even falling again. Heap clouds dying out under encroaching layer clouds. Long swell running athwart the immediate seaway. Possibly confused sea	All the signs of another frontal depression with wind from typically S or SW, low cloud. Rapid advance of leaden sky. Barometer falling fast. Wind rising	When bad weather follows bad weather that has just passed, then it usually does so by means of a secondary depression. This often rapidly follows the one that has just gone. The signs listed are those for this form of marked and rapid deterioration. It is often made dangerous because of the rapidity with which the wind rises, by the cross sea that develops and by the fact that it is normal to assume that better weather is sure to follow bad weather

Local winds are of immense importance to yachtsmen, for they are winds of the coastline and the shoreline. They are the winds that modify the gradient winds when the latter are light to moderate, which is when most people sail for pleasure. Lakes fill geologic gouges between mountains, so local slope winds are in many cases dominant on such waters. Waterways of any kind steer the gradient wind along them. Thus it is that wherever people sail, the local winds will be their constant companions and often a source of frustration. Here is a description of the more important local winds.

Sea breezes blow by day from coastal waters to the land in spring and summer in most latitudes. They often produce the highest frequency of winds at coastal places in temperate latitudes at these seasons and they are not unknown in autumn as well. We cannot preclude them in lower latitudes in good spells of winter (or cool season) weather. As they are so important the sea breezes are covered in detail (46–51) and help in forecasting them is given in table form (52).

Nocturnal winds are local winds that blow at night from the land to the sea when gradient winds are light or gentle. The term nocturnal wind is coined to include two different coastal wind-making forces that operate at night (58) (Fig. 4). These are:

Land breezes that blow from the land as it cools below the sea temperature at night. Plus

Katabatic winds that sink off coastal slopes when the sun has forsaken them. As the land rises away from the coast in most places (Holland and the Everglades are notable exceptions) it is always on the cards that a wind from the land at night is katabatic plus land breeze and the term 'nocturnal wind' includes both causes.

Anabatic winds are the reverse of katabatics in that they flow uphill when slopes previously in shadow are illuminated by the sun. They assist sea breezes but are not as important in this role as katabatics are in assisting nocturnal winds.

Mountain and Valley winds are the result of differential heating and cooling of mountain slopes and will be experienced inland on lakes that lie in mountainous regions. They are the complex effects of anabatics by day and katabatics at evening, guided by the topography of the mountains and valleys (110).

Steered winds are winds whose direction (and often speed as well) has been significantly altered by being forced to flow at angles off shores, or across promontories or on to bays. Channelways such as rivers, estuaries and creeks will provide steered winds and these winds are often modified to a considerable scale. The steering is normally a tendency to follow the shoreline more closely than the original wind would have done.

Inland on lakes, rivers, reservoirs etc. there will be no land breeze, as that is a phenomenon of the coast, but katabatics will sink off slopes that lose the sun early. Any local steep slope that was in the sun and is now in shadow is a potential source of a katabatic wind sinking on to the water. The katabatic is a smooth-flowing, ground-hugging wind that will seek the easiest path to the water, skirting spurs and seeking valleys. It will even be deflected by sizeable local clumps of trees or shoreside buildings. The same remarks apply to the land breeze, which may often not exceed 100 ft (30 metres) in depth. Nocturnal winds can blow more often than might be imagined from the strength of the daytime wind. This is because wind speed falls over the land at evening and the light weather days that are succeeded by nights with nocturnal wind, often go almost completely calm in the evening before the nocturnal wind sets in.

Coasts that are good 'sea breeze coasts' (46), (50) are also in most cases coasts with a maximum of nocturnal winds. The land breeze rarely exceeds 6 knots, but with steep local slopes the added strength of the katabatic can produce 10 to 15 knots

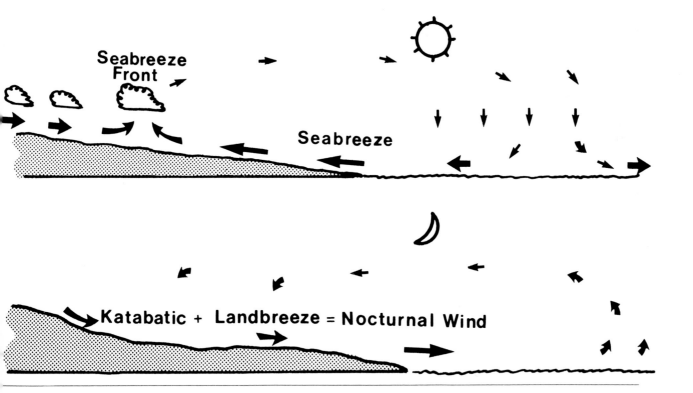

Seabreeze Front

Seabreeze

Katabatic + Landbreeze = Nocturnal Wind

39

or more sometimes. Such speeds are however rare. The nocturnal wind is, for most coasts, a light or gentle ghosting affair and coastwise, passage-making yachts need to be well inshore to take full advantage of it. Most nocturnal winds will not survive as far as 10 miles from the coast. The prospects for nocturnal wind can be assessed from (58).

Coastal slope winds are katabatics at their strongest and need mountains rising back from the sea with their tops covered in snow to achieve their maximum. When they do so, aided by an off-shore gradient wind, they often blow at gale force. The archetypal coastal slope winds are the Mistral of the Gulf of Lions and the Bora of the Adriatic. Lesser coastal slope winds will blow off any close hill slopes that have pretensions to being mountainous.

Downdraught or Falling winds are produced on steep slopes of lakes, lochs etc. (more rarely along steep sea coasts) by the sudden eruption of big showers and especially thunderstorms. They are very dangerous as gale force gusts descend the slopes ahead of the arrival of rain, replacing previously gentle wind conditions.

Thunderstorm winds are spreading fresh to gale force winds due to downdraughts brought down under intense storms. In thundery conditions wind that is light from a direction that appears to feed the coming storms will be experienced. Such winds ahead of bad storms are usually not above 10–15 knots.

Tornado winds are formed in association with thundery conditions and only a local warning service broadcast can really be said to usefully forecast them.

Tornado Storm Spouts are waterspouts formed when a tornado leaves the land for the water.

Waterspouts form under thunderstorms over the water. They are less intense than tornado storm spouts.

These notes describe most of the winds induced by storms.

Take the main coastline and divide the adjacent sea and land areas into zones parallel to it. These will be called wind zones. The diagram below will show the extent of the zones and the names we shall apply to them.

Of necessity the limits of the wind zones are rough, but they are dictated by the necessity to describe sea breeze and nocturnal wind effects in particular. The sea breeze is a complex wind, but it can be understood and rules laid down about it if the reader can first position himself in one of the zones described in Fig. 5 (42).

Offshore Zone is where the ocean racers and the deep water passage makers will sail, but very few dinghies or small cruisers will be found. It is where the wind is dictated by the gradient wind direction and the shifts will be due to pressure patterns changing. However, sometimes when conditions are right sea breeze effects will extend into the offshore zone.

Coastwise Zone is the region where most passage makers will be found as they cruise the coast from one haven to the next. It is a zone where sea breeze effects will reach on many days when they are active over the coast itself. It is on the edge of the realm of the nocturnal wind and it will be very rare for steered winds to really affect the wind this far out.

Inshore Zone is where dinghies which sail off the beach, or which are competing on an Olympic-type course, or which are just 'outside' for a spin, will be found. It is the zone that many small cruisers and powerboats will frequent. It is also the zone with a maximum chance of wind shift at most times of the day or night. Here sea breezes are born and from this zone they extend their influence seaward and landward with the day. Steered winds will be prevalent here when close to the shore itself. Nocturnal winds will reach their maximum strength and frequency in this zone.

Beachlands Zone is that zone of the coastal land mass that lies directly inland from the shore. It includes the coastal creeks and harbours that probably contain the bulk of the sailing fraternity's activities. It is often a coastal plain with backing hills and the latter may be ten or more miles inland. Here is where the sea breeze will blow if it is going to. Sometimes it never gets farther inland than this zone, although it is perhaps more normal for it to get 15–20 miles (20–30 km) inland on most occasions when the strength of the gradient wind allows it to blow at all.

Like the inshore zone there is a maximum chance of wind shift in the beachlands zone, both from sea breeze and nocturnal wind effects as well as other causes.

Coastal Zone is chosen as it is far enough inland for effects borne on onshore sea winds to have established overland characteristics, such as gustiness, that they did not possess over the sea. It is also where the sea breeze frontal system will have had time to organize itself when sea breezes set in against offshore winds. Other effects like showers formed over warm coastal sea that arrive over cooler land at night, will not have died out in the few miles from the coastline, but on the whole the coastal zone is land and is not dictated to by the adjacent sea.

Inland Zone is the true land where sea winds will have lost most of their oceanic characteristics. It is also the zone into which sea breezes penetrate only when the conditions are good, although the seaward side of the zone will often have sea breezes. It will also experience the curious alternations between calm and fitful wind that are to be found under sea breeze fronts that have reached the limit of their penetration. When conditions are good the sea breeze system will penetrate inland for tens of miles, possibly 50 miles on the best days. Apart from that the inland zone is dominated by land winds or sea winds that have developed the convection currents that are so often to be found over the land in daytime.

8m.   **SEA**   2m.   Coast Line   3m.   **LAND**   10m.

Offshore)   Coastwise   Inshore Beachlands   Coastland   Inland

Anyone who drifts about in conditions verging on flat calm in the morning knows he can expect to have some wind by the afternoon. This is because of the normal change in wind speed that occurs with the day and is called the **diurnal variation.**

The diurnal variation follows the sun. When the sun is high then so is the wind speed and when the sun begins to go down, so does the speed of the wind. Wind speed on the coast tends to be lowest just after the sun has gone down and just before sunrise.

Low cloud—particularly of the cumulus type—also tends to follow the same patterns. Clear cool mornings become full of Cu by the afternoon, but the Cu tends to die with evening and there is often a clear night. In settled weather higher clouds also tend to increase with the day although the rule is not so well obeyed for them.

Both the increase in wind speed and of cloud are linked to the heating of the land by the sun. No similar variation occurs over the ocean. Wind speed increases with height in the lower layers of the atmosphere. Friction slows the wind near the surface. When Cu clouds form, it shows that the lower layers are being mixed so that faster wind from aloft can speed up the wind in the sailing layer. So the wind is bound to increase when Cu forms and when Cu dies so the mixing stops, friction takes over and the wind mutes.

Thus the wind's day is dictated firstly by local heating or cooling of the land. This makes the speed rise with the day and fall at night. It also makes the sea breezes blow near the coast; lake winds and mountain and valley winds blow inland both by day and by night. Near the coast the nocturnal wind blows by night.

Secondly, the wind's day is dictated by the gradient windspeed. Too much gradient wind and local winds are over-ridden, although the diurnal speed change is evident even in sustained gradient winds as high as Force 6–8. However, winds due to travelling pressure systems rise and fall at odd times that do not fit the diurnal variation. Such unusual risings or fallings of the wind indicate that the pressure pattern is changing locally.

The table shown is compiled for those days when most yachtsmen are happy to be out, when there is not too much wind and some sunshine, or at least broken skies. To use the table choose a time and place and see what influences there may be on the wind. Then consult the more detailed sections for further information.

The Wind's Day

Temperate Latitudes with wind strengths between calm and 15 kts. Summer half of the year, e.g. April to October inclusive.
'Morning wind' refers to the wind that gets up after dawn but before sea breezes blow.
Choose time and place and see what the wind might be doing. Fresh winds are not much modified by local wind effects other than

Inland Zone more than 10 miles inland	Dawn calms or time of lightest wind speed	Overnight inversion breaks over the land and wind appears at the surface. Gradient wind blows and increases to maximum by 1500				
					Sea breeze blows on the best sea breeze days	
	Valley winds blow from mountains		Valley winds blow towards mountains			
Coastal Zone between 3–4 and 10 miles inland	Dawn calms or time of lightest winds	Morning wind may pick up from calm	Morning wind (gradient wind) established and increases with time. Sea breeze shifts occur when morning is calm		Gradient wind blows but sea breeze can replace it. Sea breeze blows if morning wind 8 kt or less	
Beachland Zone to between 3–4 miles inland	Dawn calms or time of lightest winds. Last of nocturnal wind	Morning wind or sea breeze drift if flat calm	Morning wind if over 8–10 kt. Sea breeze shifts if 1–5 kt.		Gradient wind if 12–15 knots. Sea breeze blows if morning wind lighter than 10 kt. (sea breeze conditions must obtain)	
	Any strong wind is gradient					

MAIN COASTLINE	04	Local Solar Time	06	08	10	12	14

Inshore Zone to about 2 miles offshore	Dawn calms. Time of lightest wind if from landward	Morning wind if from land. Otherwise maintains gradient	Sea breeze calms when light or gentle wind from landward. Sea breeze begins to blow by end of period if land wind less than 4–6 kt		Sea breeze blows. or other wind direction shifted towards land. Onshore winds increased by sea breeze effect. Fitful calms if morning wind 10–15 kt.	
	Still nocturnal wind?					
Coastwise Zone between 2 and 8–10 miles offshore	Gradient wind (from seaward or landward). Nocturnal wind (landward only)		Gradient wind blows but some sea breeze 'holes' in the wind ———— on inshore edge of the zone		Sea breeze picks up and blows unless gradient too strong (12–15 kt)	
		Morning wind from landward picks up and probably shifts				
Offshore Zone more than 10 miles offshore	Gradient wind probably light if from landward		Gradient wind is only possible wind unless morning absolutely flat calm. Then onshore drift possible by end of period		Sea breeze may produce calms and then shift later in period on good sea breeze days	

Note. Winds due to intense systems like thunderstorms, tornadoes and hurricanes though rare, can occur at any time of day or night and take over any existing wind regime.

steering by topography. Moderate winds are on the edge of being altered by sea breezes and not usually at all by nocturnal winds. Otherwise effects are greatest in fair conditions.

Sea breeze can blow up to 40–50 miles inland on some evenings. Otherwise gradient wind will blow but falls in speed	Katabatic winds blow in hilly districts. Otherwise gradient wind will blow. Lighter than during the day. Increasing gradient often means stronger wind by tomorrow	
Thunderstorm winds at their most probable	Valley winds blow from mountains	
Sea breeze may blow. Calms can be due to sea breeze fronts. Gradient wind if above 15 kt.	Gradient winds lighten. Calms follow daytime sea breezes before onset of nocturnal wind. Latter by end of period	Nocturnal winds blow but falter by end of period sometimes leading to dawn calms. Gradient winds blow at their lightest
Sea breeze blows for a time but falters and may go calm by end of period	Early night calms or light winds. Nocturnal wind by end of period (if stronger than gradient wind)	Nocturnal winds blow at their strongest (gentle to moderate) but falter towards dawn. If stronger then gradient wind—any onshore wind is gradient
	Nocturnal winds blow more strongly on steep coasts	

16	18	20	22	24	02	04

Sea breeze still blows at first, then falters. Coastal calms, picking up to gradient wind if any. Any increasing wind is usually gradient	Early night calms or light winds. Nocturnal wind by end of period. Any wind other than nocturnal wind is gradient wind	Nocturnal winds blow at thier strongest. Any wind off the sea is gradient A more than gentle wind from the land means gradient + nocturnal
Sea breeze falters and dies to fitful calms. Followed by gradient wind if any	Gradient wind or nocturnal wind by end of period	Nocturnal wind blows at a few knots. Otherwise gradient wind (but at its lightest). Dawn calms occur towards end of period
Sea breeze occasionally blows and falters to temporary calm. Otherwise gradient wind	Gradient wind. A very light gradient can become switched to nocturnal wind on clear nights. Normally, however, only gradient wind	

Almost without exception coasts experience daytime winds from the sea called sea breezes.

The Beachland and Inshore zones of the coast, where the majority of people sail, experience most sea breezes. When the wind is from a point inland, or even parallel to the coastline, then extensive wind shifts occur. The important tactical situation to recognize is the one when a sea breeze frontal system will be formed. Then typical wind shifts as the front passes across Beachland or Coastal waterways on its way inland are, for example:

On an east-facing coast: W 3–5 knots before, suddenly shifting to SE 5–8 knots and strengthening to most 10–15 knots by mid afternoon. On a south-facing coast: NW 5–8 knots in the morning, shifting in 2 minutes to SSW 10–12 knots, but this shift not occurring until the afternoon.

These are just typical of the transformations of tactical situation that sea breezes can produce and many kinds of variations are possible. In the tables (52) and (53) it is assumed that the typical sea breeze day is involved. Hints on possible variations are given but not every sea breeze is predictable in time or place. However, *some* are and by following the hints on days and wind speeds it should be possible to recognize those days that are almost certain to produce a breeze. Then one can keep an eye out for it so as to meet it when it comes.

A sea breeze day is one where nature conspires to make the breeze possible. It has bright blue skies early and for best results Cu clouds develop. The wind is less than 8 knots over the land (10–12 knots over the sea) and big shifts come when the morning wind blows from the land to the sea.

Sea breeze fronts, like miniature cold fronts, form between a light or gentle wind blowing off the land in the morning and the sea breeze starting to blow from the sea (Fig. 3 (39)). Such a front is recognized by a line of cloud along it (55) and (94).

On dry days it may form the only cloud in the vicinity of the coast. On other days when Cu clouds form readily the sea breeze front divides the coastal sky in half. To seaward it is usually quite cloudless, to landward fleets of Cu clouds. The sea-breeze fronts on sea breeze coasts form more or less continuous lines parallel to the coast and move inland at about 3 knots at first, increasing to 6–8 knots in the afternoon. Thus the front rolls back the offshore wind, producing wind shifts that are amongst the widest experienced. They may indeed be 180° shifts and occur almost instantaneously, the light wind from the land suddenly being replaced by the somewhat stronger breeze from the sea.

At other times the mode of onset is not so sharp and there is a calm patch between the two winds. For example craft can, at the same time
1. be beating into the breeze on the seaward side,
2. be running before the wind in the same direction on the landward side and
3. be listlessly becalmed under the sea breeze front itself.

To be sailing or racing on waters just inland from the coastline and to recognize the sea breeze front advancing from the coast is to have advance knowledge of a wind shift, the final direction of which is often almost precisely known as it frequently comes from a direction some 20° to the left of the direct onshore line. It is also a wind without useful tactical windshifts in it (64).

Coastal wind shifts that are due to sea breeze influence occur on many summer days. Examples are when fresh winds blow nearly parallel to a coastline. These are too strong to be shifted fully to blow on shore, but a shorewards cant occurs as the day progresses.

Onshore morning winds on sea breeze days are reinforced by the breeze and it is prudent to consider the wind speed

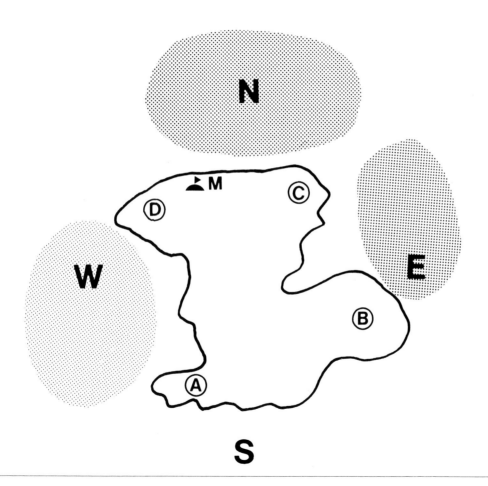

(see page 108)

47

doubling during the afternoon. The wind may also shift more nearly to the onshore direction.

Sea breeze coasts are mainly east-facing and south-facing coasts which have extensive coastal plains backed by low hills. Here the sea breeze frontal systems form most readily and move farthest inland. Sea breezes are also drawn from far to seaward. With prevailing westerly winds many sea breeze frontal situations must occur on these coasts, thus they are also coasts of strong probability of daytime wind shifts.

Sea breeze wind speed is 10–15 knots at maximum in latitudes of about 40–60° N, but may reach 25–30 knots in sub-tropical latitudes.

Sea breeze afternoons are when the breeze will slowly alter its direction to blow more from the left of the direct onshore direction.

Sea breeze evenings are often calm or very light, but later a nocturnal wind will set in from the land (58).

Sea breeze Effects to Seaward

The sea breeze Inshore comes earliest of anywhere. It is here that the wind from the land falls to calm in the forenoon before the sea breeze gets going. Shifts occur here that may not be experienced a few miles to seaward or inland.

The sea breeze Coastwise starts slowly and later than Inshore—perhaps by early or even late afternoon. The wind goes calm before picking up slowly from seaward.

The sea breeze Offshore is more rarely experienced in temperate latitudes, but is prevalent in lower latitudes.

The way the sea breeze system works in place and time has been extensively covered and in greater detail than here. Firstly, in *Wind and Sailing Boats* and secondly, in *The Wind Pilot*. In the latter the complexities of the system have been somewhat simplified by the use of the 'sea breeze carpet' analogy.

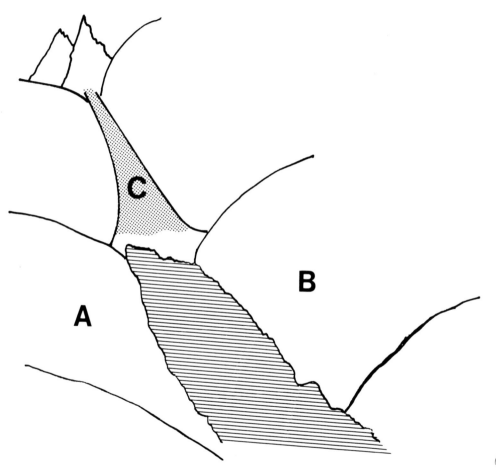

(see page 110)

Below is a resumé of the shifts etc. that sea breeze effects produce in the various zones parallel to the coastline. On the left are the variations that usually happen to a wind that blows from the land to the sea within an arc of 70° either side of the direct line inland from the main sea coast.

Wind in the morning from the land

Inland	Sea breeze shifts occur middle of the afternoon and into the evening, if at all. On good sea breeze days (light winds and Cu clouds) sea breeze front advances from coast as long as sun provides power and convection can continue. Morning shifts are due: 1. to establishment of gradient wind (9), 2. to local thermal influences (108). Other afternoon shifts may be due to local storms, showers etc. Evening gradient wind re-established after a quiet period
Coastal	Sea breeze shifts early afternoon to late afternoon. Off-shore wind rolled back and reversed behind a calm zone (sea breeze front) (56). Early shifts can be establishment of gradient wind after dawn calms or in flat calm, anabatic drift to inland hills. Evening gradient wind re-established only after calm period in most cases
Beachlands	Sea breeze shifts late forenoon or early afternoon. Calm areas formed during establishment of sea breeze front over beach move inland. Sea breeze cannot pull in from seaward until sea breeze front forms and moves. Many sea breeze effects in this zone. Normal loss of sea breeze to a calm evening but can re-establish gradient suddenly.
Coastline	~~~~~~
Inshore	Morning wind calms and then pulls back towards beach in early forenoon if morning wind is light, in later forenoon if gentle wind (10). The most likely zone for wind shifts due to sea breeze effects. Gradient not usually re-established before evening after calm period
Coastwise	Sea breeze shifts spread into zone in early afternoon to late afternoon. Wind usually goes calm for a period and then pulls in towards shore. This calm zone moves out towards offshore as day progresses. Gradient re-established in evening after calm period
Offshore	Sea breeze shifts in middle afternoon to early evening but only in light weather. Event is fairly rare in temperate latitudes. Less rare farther south. Light on-shore breeze can be established up to 20-30 miles offshore. Light airs in evening or near calm followed by re-established gradient wind direction

On the right are the shifts that usually occur when the morning wind is within 20° either side of the main sea coastline. The events are those associated with sea breeze coasts that are only indented by headlands and inlets, bays etc. to a depth of about 10 miles and have a flattish hinterland that rises to coastal hills. Other venues, where high ground comes close to the sea, where coastline takes a sharp turn for tens of miles, where lagoons, etangs etc. go many miles inland, may not obey the rules. On-shore wind direction is not covered as only predictable effects are a swing to more on-shore and an increase in speed

Morning wind within 20° either side of main coastline direction

Sea breeze shifts middle of the afternoon to early evening. A swing of direction more from seaward can be carried into this zone but only in light to gentle winds. Any such tendency will revert to gradient wind again by evening. Other influences on the morning wind are as opposite

Sea breeze shifts occur early afternoon to late afternoon. Light to gentle morning wind shifts more towards seaward direction and increases. If moderate wind there can be a shift, but not marked

Sea breeze swings off the sea during forenoon or early afternoon. Light wind swings in and increases in strength. Gentle wind swings slowly to normal sea breeze direction but may not get there fully. Moderate wind may come in from 40° to seaward of coastline direction but often much nearer to coastline direction

Sea breeze swings off the sea in early forenoon if light wind; later forenoon if gentle wind; afternoon if moderate wind. Wind shifts to sea breeze direction, either all at once or in a series of swings. Complex shifts occur when wind moderates

Shift occurs to more directly onshore at inshore edge of this zone in early afternoon to late afternoon. Only rarely does effect extend to offshore zone. If wind moderate then possibly no effect at all

Only light to gentle morning winds see the effects translated 20 miles out and then not before middle afternoon to early evening. Possibility of shift more directly landward as day progresses but early evening return to gradient wind direction

Will There be a Sea Breeze?

Photo 8 *(p. 54)*
A typical sea breeze day looking up an estuary on the south coast of England. Here is a morning with the look that says 'sea breeze!'. The wind is light and there are Cu clouds in the sky, but the sun can still get to the land. There will surely be a sea breeze soon.

To assess the possibility of a sea breeze from forecast or actual conditions, first choose your sailing area. ↓ means that a sea breeze is probable (↓ that it is possible) so move down to next section. Then assess actual or forecast wind speed. Next, cloud cover and finally, if sea breeze has proved possible with the combination of conditions, from the wind direction assess the way the breeze may set in.

Sailing area	Offshore	Coastwise	Inshore	Beachland	Coastal	Inland
	10 m. off (a) **No**	3–10 m. off ↓	0–2 m. off ↓	0–4 m. inland ↓	4–20 m. inland ↓	20 m. inland (b) **No**
Wind speed (assessed at about 0900)	Force 0–2 Calm to light 0–6 kt ↓		Force 3–4 Gentle to mod. 7–16 kt ↓		Force 5–6 Fresh to strong 17–27 kt (c) **No**	Force 7–8 Gale 28+ kt **No**
Cloud cover	Sunny (fine) ↓	Sunny periods Bright periods (d)↓	Sunny intervals Bright intervals (d)↓		Cloudy (e) **No**	Overcast (dull) (f) **No**
Wind direction (assessed at about 0900)	From mainland ← sea breeze frontal system (46), (50)		Parallel to main sea coast sea breeze frontal system if Force 0–2. Shift to seaward if Force 3–4 (50)		From seaward → increase in strength and possibly shift more from seaward (50)	

The above establishes the prospects for or against a sea breeze. Forecast or actual weather conditions may assist or hamper the establishment of a sea breeze. If the above shows, in the forenoon, that the sea breeze is likely then consult the following:

Weather	Small Cu clouds	Showers	Thunderstorms	Fog/poor visibility	Rain/drizzle	Increase in high cloud	Increase in wind
	If over coastlands then the Cu assists	Inland can assist if not fierce. Over coast may kill sea breeze	In forenoon and early afternoon sweep away sea breeze which can return later	Hinders sea breeze. Sluggish coastal calms	Kills sea breeze. Slackens it if light intermittent	Damps sea breeze at first. Kills it later if continuous cloud build-up	Blows away sea breeze if Force 4 or more

Notes.
a. Possible landward drift on calm mornings. Maybe moderate by midday in low latitudes.
b. Inland drift on calm mornings is not sea breeze, but plains wind.
c. If in lower latitudes just possible. So continue to next section.
d. 'periods' = more sun than cloud; 'intervals' = more cloud than sun.
e. If warmth can be felt through cloud and wind is already calm to light, then breeze can come. If very light, allow for thin cloud to clear on summer mornings.
f. If overcast on coast, but it looks bright inland then sea breeze can be drawn in when wind light.

When to Expect a Sea Breeze Windshift—morning wind blowing from the land

Photo 9 (p. 55)
Typical cloud along a sea breeze front. The sea is off to the right and the front has just crossed the area and is moving inland (left). Note deep Cu clouds of the front itself with dark elements below. There is apparently unbroken Cu inland while there is no low cloud on this, the seaward side, of the front.

Having decided from the previous page that there is likely to be a sea breeze, it is tactically important to know when it might arrive. Thus one must recognize the signs accompanying its onset. Sea breezes rarely set in against off-shore winds that are above 8–10 knots mean speed at about 0900–1000 LST (Local Solar Time) in latitudes lying between about 40° and 60° (wind speed measured over the land). From observations made on the good sea breeze coast of southern England one can conclude that sea breezes should occur by the given LST's on most similar sea breeze coasts.

Times by which sea breeze should have occurred

Zone	Calm	Wind speed—wind from landward (i.e. off-shore): Measured at about 0900–1000 LST					
		1–2 kt	2–4 kt	4–6 kt	6–8 kt	8–10 kt	10–14 kt
Inland	Landward drift at any time	50 miles inland by 2000–2200 40 miles inland by 1900–2100 30 miles inland by 1800–2000 20 miles inland by 1600–1700	On the best sea breeze days and on good sea breeze coasts				
10 miles Coastal	1200–1300	1300–1400	1400–1500	1400–1700	Not normally possible		
	Times in this zone are for a place 10 miles inland from the main sea coast.						
4 miles Beachland	1000	1100	1200	1300–1400	1500–1600	Not normally possible	
	Times in this zone are measured at a place 3 miles inland from main sea coast. Subtract about 1–2 hours for the coastline itself						
Coastline	〰〰〰						
Inshore	Times in this zone are for between 1½ and 2 miles out from main sea coast. Add about 1 hour for coastline itself.						
	0800–0900	0830–1000	1000–1100	1100–1200	1200–1400	Often no true breeze but off-shore wind reduced in afternoon	
3 miles Coastwise	0900–1100	1100–1200	1300–1400	1400–1500	1500–1600	Often no true sea breeze but wind reduced in afternoon	
	Times in this zone are for about 10 miles from main coastline						
15 miles Offshore	1000	1300–1500	1500–1700	Wind reduced sometimes but usually no sea breeze		Usually no effect	
	Times in this zone are for about 20 miles from the main coastline						

(Contd. pp. 56, 57)

The table on page 53 suggests when the sea breeze front could arrive. Use the hints below to recognize it when it does come.

Landward Zones
Here are signs of the approaching sea breeze front, under which is the shift to the breeze from seaward. Very dry airstreams will not have clouds along the sea breeze front to mark it and make the shift visible.

Zone	In the early forenoon look for	In the next few hours look for	The sea breeze front is marked by	Ten to twenty minutes before the shift
Beachland and Coastal	Cu clouds which first develop over inland hills but later spread seaward. Allow for any cloudy—bright or misty mornings breaking up to Cu and heat	Signs of Cu not surviving over coastline and sea (sunshine on cars, boats, buildings etc. near coast itself). Cloud overhead remaining well broken—half cover or less. Off-shore wind will increase somewhat as morning progresses but lightens with approach of sea breeze front	A darker, deeper line of Cu clouds formed parallel to main coastline and advancing inland. Wind lightening to calm. Gulls, swifts or other soaring birds under cloudbase. Contrast of bright sun conditions on seaward side of the front	Wind progressively lightens. Some puffs from landward interspersed with calm and then puffs from seaward. Eventually sea breeze front moves inland leaving venue in breeze and bright sunshine
Inland	Cu day without much wind. Sea breeze takes time to travel so for 'early forenoon' above read time given in table. Cu can get quite extensive inland and still the breeze will come	Any signs to seaward of unusual amount of sunshine through haze layer below cloudbase	Above signs	As above

The sea breeze system tends to make clouds disperse over coastal waters, so making it difficult to recognize the onset of the calm that sets in (sea breeze antifront) and the breeze that follows it. Below are a few suggestions.

Zone	In the early forenoon look for	In the next few hours look for	The sea breeze antifront is marked by	Sea breeze gathers momentum
nshore	Cu clouds that first develop over inland hills and then spread seawards. The Cu shows convection that is necessary for a virile sea breeze system to develop. Broken higher cloud or any cloud that allows sun to get to the land will be allied to a sea breeze	Signs that the off-shore wind is lightening—certainly it should not be increasing markedly. Cu clouds tending to die out so that it becomes sunnier	Falling of off-shore wind to calm. Curious shell-shaped catspaws round a craft due to sinking jets. These darken the water just as wind does, but there is no horizontal wind yet. Clear sky overhead. Fitful and often very light puffs towards shore	When sea breeze front forms over beach. Look for bigger darker Cu forming line over beach. Then expect the slight on-shore drift to pick up soon to a 4–6 kt or more onshore breeze
oastwise	Same as above	Can be as above on landward side of this zone and conditions will spread seawards with time	Above signs progressively later, the farther from shore	This zone needs the real sea breeze front to develop before it can expect breeze

Will There be a Nocturnal Wind?

Photo 10 *(p. 62)*
The kind of evening when a nocturnal wind before midnight is almost certain. It is obviously flat calm in this coastal river mooring and there cannot be much more breeze in the open. There are totally clear skies, so the land can cool by radiation. What cannot be seen as we are looking seaward is that there are hills inland that will add their katabatic drift to the land breeze current.

Nocturnal wind will be the accompaniment to any coast in quiet weather. Statistics show that on average in the summer half of the year most coastal places experience a preponderance of winds off the land during the night. Thus inshore and coastwise cruising craft should expect and make use of the nocturnal wind. The table below shows how to forecast its onset from the strength

Forecast or actual weather at sunset	Off a coast that is	Wind speed at sunset
Clear sky with normal visibility. Sun sets visibly, i.e. little obscuring low cloud. Any low cloud should be dispersing. High clouds should not show signs of increasing rapidly. In other words, every sign of a fair night	Flat coastal plain backed by hills	Calm or light air 0–3 kt
The above weather regime that allows radiation to cool the land and the hill slopes is essential. If coast faces E or S then sun has left the nearer hill slopes a long time before sun sets in summer. Thus early katabatics	As above but this speed and higher can be replaced by nocturnal wind when steep hill and mountain slopes come behind the coastal plain	Light breeze 4–6 kt
All the radiation stops must be out if this wind speed is to be affected. Cool clear nights are possible candidates so long as wind is not tending to increase	Big hill ridges backing the coastal plain but within a few miles of it. However, mountains farther back will provide moderate nocturnal winds and keep them going into the early morning. Possibly as late as the early forenoon	Gentle breeze 7–10 kt
A clear night and this wind speed at sunset must preclude nocturnal wind except as an additive to an already off-shore wind	Only coastal-slope winds as experienced in the Mediterranean can really influence this wind speed	Moderate breeze 11–16 kt

f an opposing wind, i.e. a light to gentle wind from sea to land.

is essential that land cools below sea temperature. Thus late summer and autumn preferred.

Prospects for nocturnal wind	Tactical comments	What can prevent it?
Almost certain to occur. Expect present wind to lighten still further to temporary calm if it is now onshore. Then to pick up by midnight slowly from landward. If wind now off-shore expect some lightening at first but no full loss of wind before nocturnal wind picks up with the night	Seek the shore as far as is prudent to achieve maximum advantage from nocturnal wind. Allow for 'holes' in the wind off cliffs and local high places and for local enhancement of strength through funnelling out of estuaries and coastal valleys etc.	Forecast of gathering wind during the night. Such wind may not become evident for some hours and then arrive suddenly sweeping away any nocturnal wind that has occurred. Gathering cloud over the land, cutting off radiation to the sky
Can occur because the wind over the land lulls with the night and so land breezes and katabatics can take over. Expect nocturnal wind late, i.e. after midnight	Above applies but the 'sunset' wind should stay longer than in above case. Changeover calm period or shift to nocturnal wind should come some hours after dark	This wind speed may be the commencement of a 'gradient' wind. Look for signs of encroaching cloud, fall of barometer etc. If so, present wind may strengthen with the night and no nocturnal wind occur
Cannot usually occur with normal coastal plain shoreline. However, if 'sunset' wind is blowing on-shore the wind over the land will be less and even this speed cannot fully rule out the chance of a nocturnal wind later in the night. However, if it occurs allow for it being swept away again before dawn or just after. If wind already off-shore then go for strengthening with the night	There is enough speed here to keep the present regime going for a long time. Possibly all night. It is touch-and-go with this wind speed whether there will be any marked shift with the night. If there is it usually means a change of speed as well. Dropping if wind is on-shore, increasing if wind is already off-shore	Simply, this speed can keep nocturnal winds out. However, coastal slope winds from steep sides close to the shoreline can easily upset the normal run of events
Very little prospect unless wind drops with the night. Forecast?	Sail as you will. A wind from the land will strengthen near the shore so stay there. If already off-shore then go anywhere	No! What can allow it? A gradient wind that lightens rapidly with the night

Where Will There be Local Wind Shifts?

Photo 11 *(p. 63)*
Rivers and estuaries produce many local wind shifts. Winds can blow round hills like the one in the background and then be altered by shoreside trees. A sheet of higher cloud, as here, limits gusts but the Cu below shows that convection currents are still occurring. So local wind shifts can occasionally be over-ridden by gusts from above.

Only hints on what to look for can be given. Each site must be judged on its form of shoreline and the direction of the wind with respect to the shoreline and the state of stability of the airstream (gusty or not). Local wind shifts are due to objects in the way of the wind or to local heating and cooling in light airs.
Most of the remarks apply to all wind zones

Type of shore	Shifts can be due to
Flat or gently rising, some trees but mainly open. Usually backed by coastal plain or other flattish hinterland. If in doubt use these remarks for small-water shores	Local thermals or sinking jets of air in calm or light air conditions
	Steering (more parallel to the shore) of wind that is already somewhat parallel to the shore
	Refractive bending to bring wind more directly off the shore when its direction is already fairly close to the perpendicular to the shoreline
	Steering of off-shore wind (0–15 kt) by shore topography when conditions are meteorologically stable, such as in the evening—night—early morning, or days with total cover of low overcast (St) cloud. Any form of Cu cloud makes for a day where the local steering effects are less noticeable
Steep-to shores and those closely backed by cliffs etc. See also (108) and (110) for lake winds	Local thermals as above. There can also be more extensive anabatic winds towards slopes in the sun and katabatic winds from slopes that have lost the sun
	Steering, which along steep shores is very marked. Refractive bending, that is very likely to affect katabatics flowing from the shore
	Mountain and valley winds (make local inquiries). See (110)
	Thunderstorm winds (downdraught or falling winds)
Wooded shores that are unavoidable and lie in the path of the wind. Also sheds, ships, houses etc. which you have to closely approach	Barriers to the wind. These may alter direction but most importantly they cut speed. Tree-lined banks with some gaps in them produce lowest speed at 5 tree heights (h) off. Wind returns to near normal at greater than 20 h. Dense woods and close-packed buildings have lowest wind speed close to them. Wind then climbs back to normal value beyond 20 h
	Gaps between dense barriers increase speed and alter direction. Wind across the waterway compressed between barriers must spread out when released and so fans across the waterway

60

ug the shallows with centreboard well up to catch the odd thermal puffs that are drawn towards a heated shoreline of mudflats or nd and shingle. This is flat calm sailing. Farther off the shore there are often complementary sinking jets of air that darken the water with a mirage of non-existent wind

Wind on-shore—tack before you are forced to do so by the shallows.
Wind off-shore—hang on right into shore

Wind on-shore—hang on
Wind off-shore—tack off the shore

ook for the gaps and valleys down which the wind will come, or up which it must go. Gusts over-ride the topographic teering so gust air will come from somewhere near the gradient direction (direction the low clouds are moving) and when the ust dies the wind will revert to being steered by the terrain

ind on-shore wind along sunlit shore in morning but not along shaded shore. Find off-shore wind along shadowed shore in vening (katabatics at this time but not anabatics). For example, if waterway orientated N–S, cant towards W shore in the forenoon nd E shore in the afternoon

Wind will tend to blow along enclosed waterways one way or the other, even when the gradient is at a wide angle to the axis f the waterway. Steering of wind by the terrain is very marked and may be dominant on lakes and rivers set between high ground

n general winds flow up valleys to mountains by day and from the mountains to the valleys by night

hunderstorms produce extreme downdraught gusty winds that fall down slopes on to the water below. Very dangerous when they occur

it top of thumb (above knuckle) at arm's length to shoreside hamper to judge 20 h. Keep this distance off and still have 80 per cent f undisturbed wind speed.
Avoid minimum wind speed at 5 h, this distance can be judged by fitting distance between thumb and forefinger of outstretched hand t arm's length to shoreside trees etc.
here is more wind close to a shore half-fronted with trees than at 5 h

Where gaps between dense barriers occur allow for increase of wind speed by funnelling

MICRO WIND SHIFTS: The Quality of the Wind

Photo 12 *(p. 66)*
The several Cu and Cb pictures scattered through the text illustrate the sky in gust cell and shower cell conditions. When a full cover of closely packed Cu occurs (Sc) some aspects of the gust cell pattern may still exist, but the pattern can be very jumbled.

Thus a sky like this can often mean that wind tactics are largely ineffective. You will have to play the shifts as they come, and there is little hope of getting into phase with a pattern.

The **quality of the wind** is a term that describes how the wind varies as it blows. It always has a mean direction and speed, and when the forecast says 'westerly, Force 4' it refers only to the mean wind direction and speed. But sailing boats never get a steady wind and to them the mean wind is only useful as a guide. It is the wind's quality that has to be sailed through as it shifts and changes speed.

Winds that have quality are either tactical or non-tactical. To be **tactical** an airstream must show some form of recurrent pattern so that a measure of anticipation of the shifts can be made by the helmsman. The shifts must also be of sufficient duration in each phase of the pattern to make it advantageous to tack on them. That means in practice a minute or two or more in each phase of the pattern.

Normal wind quality comes from **gust cells**. These are separate entities moving in the wind field and usually capped by Cu clouds. Meteorological considerations lead to a veered (clockwise) shift, and a gust at the head of a gust cell under the leading edge of the capping Cu cloud. As the cloud passes the veered phase relaxes in speed and backs (anticlockwise shift) until the wind has lulled under the trailing edge of the Cu element. The next gust cell follows the lull with a gust and a veer and the pattern repeats. Gust cells can occur even in dry airstreams where no Cu clouds result, and in fact most airstreams show some aspects of the normal shift pattern. It is, however, at its maximum of effectiveness when the sky is populated by Cu clouds and the wind is about Force 3–5.

The gust cell pattern is over-ridden when Cu clouds grow big enough to produce **showers**. Then the wind will back ahead and veer behind the passage of the big Cu or there may be a line of them stretched across the wind. The shift pattern is then one of 15–30 minutes duration and each shower has its own shower cell of wind shift below it.

(In Southern Hemisphere for 'veer' read 'back' and vice versa.)

On days when temperature inversions exist and convection is inhibited an **abnormal shift pattern** is engendered in the wind. The attributes of the abnormal pattern are covered on (72). The gust cell idea now cannot be used, but the abnormal pattern often shows variability which, as well as having tactical attributes that are the exact opposite of the normal, is high in the scale of variability.

These are the three tactical wind patterns that can be recognized in the present state of our knowledge. Others may exist but recognizing them is far more difficult than the ones listed above.

Non-tactical airstreams are those in which no recurrent pattern occurs. The largely random shifts have to be met and countered each on its merits and anticipation is largely impossible. Also in this group are the very steady wind streams that include sea breezes and land breezes. An increase in wind speed from moderate to fresh can turn what was a tactical airstream into a non-tactical one, because the size of the turbulent eddies in the wind begins to swamp the convective eddies that formed the gust cells.

Below is a table which gives a scale of variability applicable to shift patterns with which the helmsman has to contend.

Scale of Variability

Variability tends to be maximum   1. in the early forenoon   2. in winds with a land fetch

Described as	Description	Particularly associated with
High	Shifts are wide, i.e. possibly 60°–90° between extreme directions. Often abnormal variability (72)	Warmth, mainly clear skies but poor visibility—days with sunshine and islands of upper cloud—sultry conditions ahead of thundery outbreaks—period before onset of sea breezes against the morning wind—E wind directions
Moderate	Shifts are 30–40° or less and often half this at sea with a sea fetch. Usually normal tactical variability	Cool polar airstreams and good visibility—Cu, or Cb and passing showers—sometimes clear skies in a dry airstream—NW wind direction is typical
Low	Shifts are small and usually random in time. Flow may be almost without turbulence in the evening and during the night	Overcast days—continuous rain sometimes mixed with showers (but not showers and bright periods as above)—evenings and nights of settled weather—very early morning before sun can heat land. When sun takes effect expect onset of high or moderate variability—any direction
Random	Shifts are dictated by wind speed and degree of atmospheric stability. Fresh winds can have moderate random variability—scale increases with increasing 'lumpiness' of skyscape	Low overcast and cyclonic weather generally—above moderate winds but wholly cloudy airstreams show random shifts with lighter winds—no sign of 'organization' in the airstream as occurs with Cu clouds—S or SW wind direction

The reaction to a shift pattern of any scale is dictated by the necessity to tack on heading shifts. This technique is applicable in all variable airstreams provided you are prepared to be caught out now and again by turbulent eddies that only last for long enough to settle on the new tack and then shift back again, demanding a new tack. The tactical airstreams to be described can be visualized in their variability and therefore some form of prediction is possible. Instead of tacking on ephemeral headers you tack therefore to the pattern that you know from the look of the day will be coming along every few minutes.

The normal tactical airstream is one associated with convection currents and thus with cumulus-type clouds. Its tactical attribute is that the wind tends to veer as it gusts and back when it lulls.

Recognition points	Typical variability
Blue skies populated with small Cu clouds (14) and (18) are good examples. Wind not too strong, i.e. mean speed of less than 15–18 knots is normal. Shift pattern is still there in stronger unstable airstreams but the pattern is not so well marked. (Includes days with Ci cloud (54), but not Cu below gathering medium level cloud (26). Nor turbulence cloud that looks like Cu (23) when the wind is strong	Moderate—4 minute gust–lull sequence. Sharp speed increase when wind gusts accompanied by a veered shift. Wind holds veered direction for 1–2 min. then shifts progressively to the backed direction with corresponding fall of speed into the lull. (*Note.* 4 min. sequence is typical. It may be 3 min. or as long as 8 min., but most NW airstreams have a 4 min. sequence)
Big Cu clouds whose depth is greater than their base height from the ground (assess using thumb as a yardstick on an isolated cloud some way away) or clouds may be already producing showers. First like (67) or (78) later like (79) or (95)	Longer period sequence as clouds grow in individual size. Big Cu bring same shift pattern as above, but probably bigger gusts and variability bordering on 'high' when wind less than 12 kt. Shower clouds Cb (79) or (95) bring a 20–30 min. shift pattern. The wind often *backs* ahead of showers and veers behind them. It is rare for showers to come in an even sequence. They come in batches with long, clearer periods between
Cu grow below a higher layer of cloud (63). Upper layer shows that Cu cannot grow deeply and so little chance of showers	Moderate—the wind speed is usually fairly low, and veer and gust, back and lull pattern when present will be less distinct than when Cu develops in blue sky or under much higher clouds (35). Sometimes, as the layer exists in an inversion (and should this be on the point of breaking) an abnormal shift pattern may result
No low cloud at all. Which can occur when the airstream is too dry to form Cu clouds. Beautiful weather but not a strong tactical airstream	Low—or sometimes moderate to high, but abnormal shift pattern. It is easy to detect which. When Cu cannot form, the convection currents are inhibited and so is the shift pattern. It is often a poor version of the Cu airstream. Visibility is often poor
Sc, i.e. a layer of low Cu lumps merged together	Low but usually normal when the Sc layer is permanent. When such a layer breaks up with the sun's heat the pattern may be abnormal

Ignore days with layer clouds (especially at low level) cyclonic skies (74) and any sky where there is no sign of convection currents, i.e. no cumuliform clouds (heap clouds). These will probably have a shift pattern but it must be assessed on the spot and may well be random, especially in the first form of sky mentioned

Photo 13 (p. 67)
The big, solid, Cu elements that can only be formed by strong convection currents. Therefore under them there must be a normal tactical airstream. Each cloud element has a gust at its head and a lull at its tail, so watch the clouds moving over and make use of them.

Recognize the shift pattern	Tactical action
1. By wind speed. If now in a lull, a gust must follow. Gusts appear under leading edges of major Cu cloud elements. So look out for Cu clouds arriving overhead. A blue gap means a gust soon and a veer of wind. Wind will be around the mean speed and direction under middle of Cu elements, and will be backed and will lull under the trailing edges and in the blue break behind. 2. from reaction of other craft to windward, heeling to a coming gust etc. 3. From gust 'splash' marks on the water	When beating assume starboard tack if practicable in the gust half of the sequence and revert to port after a couple of minutes. Hold port tack into and through the lull, but be ready to resume starboard tack when wind gusts. You have perhaps 150 seconds of veered wind so waiting for 10–20 seconds to check that the first stab of the gust is not just a turbulent eddy will not lose you much and may gain a great deal from a considered tack that can be held. It is less easy to assess when to tack back on to port, but consider doing so after a couple of minutes have elapsed on the starboard tack. (In the southern hemisphere, for port read starboard and vice versa wherever it occurs)
1. By the coming cloud elements. Cu clouds must be deep to produce showers (note (95) where depth of cloud is 5 or 6 times the distance base to ground). If big Cu clouds without any showers expect enhanced pattern as above. 2. If these grow into showers then each becomes a wind-making entity in its own right. Expect heavy gusts when shower starts and a backed wind direction; 10–15 min. of bluster and downpour and then a further period with wind veering and precipitation dying out. Relatively low wind speed in the blue break behind	As above when beating and the clouds are lumpy and large, but not producing showers. Allow for a good plane under the leading edges when off the wind. When running allow for veer in the gust by assuming port tack (gybe). If big Cb shower cloud prepare to meet a 20–30 kt gust under leading edge and expect to have to weather it for at least 5–10 min. Remember to reverse the tactical rules above when big showers bring backing winds ahead and veering winds behind them
Much more chance of a mixed up shift pattern with some normal and some abnormal shift sequences. Look, however, for the individual Cu elements below the upper cloud. There will be a normal pattern of shift with them. Between clouds the shifts are less determinate	Less useful as a tactical airstream but one where it will probably pay to tack on headers rather than try to divine the shifts to come. If a pattern emerges then use it
By shift pattern. If the direction shifts widely but stays in the phases of its shifts for a period that may be measured in minutes, turn to the next pages, for this is an abnormal shift pattern. If the shift pattern is rather indistinct—if you cannot really see what it is doing—then it is probably normal verging on random	Take it as it comes. Before the start of a race try to get off on your own and sample the shift pattern
By shift pattern. It is difficult to give rules about this type of cloud cover as so many things can affect the surface wind speed and direction	Above advice applies

Photo 14 *(opposite)*
This is the form of cloud that is associated with coming thunder. The small turreted heads, often ranged in lines along the wind at their level (centre of the picture) are typical. Thicker cloud which comes with thunder often follows some hours later than the arrival of this cloud and can look like (103) at first and (86) later. It is a sky that goes with an abnormal windshift pattern.

The abnormal Tactical Airstream is one that often occurs on warm summer days where, despite the heat, Cu clouds do not readily develop. We cannot discount them being seen somewhere in the sky but this airstream is likely to look like (66) or (71) or (103). The cloud is often high and well broken up. It may seem a little thundery and the visibility will not be very good. It will often be warm or hot for the time of year and the wind will not be much above 10–15 knots and often less.

Recognition points	*Typical variability*
Not as easy to recognize as the normal airstream because it is associated with the existence of a low, temperature inversion (about 1000 m). Clouds may not form readily in the lower layers to make it recognizable. It is often associated with skies like (71) and sometimes with (103) or (66). Mornings of warm sultry days with poor visibility. The wind will not usually be above moderate	High to moderate (65). Increase–decrease sequence lasting 5–8 min having corresponding backing with the increase and veering with the decrease. (Compare the normal shift pattern.) An easterly for example, may spend a minute or more shifing progressively to, say, SE while its speed falls to a low value. It will probably then spend several minutes in this direction before shifting back progressively to, say, NE and increasing in strength to moderate. The whole sequence may last as long as 15–20 min. but 8 min. is more typical. A full 90° between phases of the pattern is probably extreme variability and perhaps 60° is more typical. In any case the shifts are so large that they cannot be ignored. It is often a phenomenon of the forenoon before the sun is high
Always consider this type of variability in the morning before or around 0800–0900 LST on sunny or fair days. Also when the inversion re-forms in late afternoon or early evening. Consider it also in the hour or so before a sea breeze front moves in against a wind off the land. It will not always be there but it can be looked for (56)	Before a sea breeze front comes in (52) and (56) consider that the wind will have phases of say 5–10 min. of back and increase in speed followed by some similar period of veer and decrease. Sometimes, however, the normal shift pattern obtains, i.e. veer and increase, and back and decrease, but the 'spikiness' of the shifts will not be like the gust–lull sequences of the normal airstream. When the sea breeze front has passed inland, expect a random airstream without much variability

The abnormality of the pattern lies on two aspects of its behaviour that are different from the normal airstream.
1. the wind backs (shifts anticlockwise) as it increases and veers (shifts clockwise) as it decreases.
2. there are two wind directions which alternately displace one another so the idea of an average or mean wind direction is not a great help.
Tactical rule: port tack when the wind increases and backs; starboard tack as it decreases and veers (compare (68)).

Recognize the shift pattern	Tactical action
By the variability and the changes in wind speed. Also by the kind of day. It is usually not a very 'fresh' day, rather humid and visibility is not at all good. The windspeed may drop almost to zero for minutes on end in some extreme cases of this form of variability. Watch the wind ashore and note how fitful it is. You may have wind from one direction for some minutes, then there suddenly seems to be little or none but a sensitive wind vane or a flag shows that the wind has markedly shifted. Watch on and off for 10 minutes or more if you can. You will then be able to recognize if this is truly an abnormal wind pattern and act accordingly	Think of the wind as two winds, one of which continually replaces the other. The phases of the pattern demand that one tacks to them because their extreme shifts are so wide. It is a kind of 'square-wave' pattern where, despite large shifts measured in seconds that must if possible be ignored, one can spend some minutes on starboard tack when the wind is lightest and most veered. Then as the wind inches its way back to the other phase of the pattern a point is reached where it is essential to tack on to port tack for the backed, stronger component of the pattern. This is a difficult wind to handle as it is always prompting one to tack on headers because there is such a large variation in 'turbulent' shifts. However, these short period shifts must be largely ignored—reacted to, but not tacked on—and the major parts of the pattern visualized and made the basis of your tactical strategy
Before a sea breeze front. There should be only small amounts of Cu and even that may not be near you when sailing near the coast. When the front does arrive the shift to sea breeze may be prolonged and very frustrating	Make the most of the tactical shifts before the sea breeze arrives. Under the sea breeze front expect frustrating puffs and calms. After the sea breeze comes in forget wind tactics and if the wind shifts, tack on headers

SAILING DAYS WITH RECOGNIZABLE WIND PATTERNS: Fair Weather—Cumulus Clouds

Main recognition points: Clear early with normal or below average temperatures for the time of year. Usually sunny and bright. Any higher cloud is usually thin and well scattered. Cu clouds develop in the forenoon over land. They should show no marked vertical development and have flat bases and rounded tops.
Possible dangers: offshore, moderate morning wind can grow to fresh or even strong by afternoon. Showers might develop with strong gusts. Otherwise a benign airstream.

Sailing venue	Time of day	Look and feel of the day	Sailing assessment
Inshore zone with off-shore wind. (Coastwise zone variations in column 7)	0800– 1200 LST	Early: clear and often cool for time of year. Good visibility for time of day. Later: Cu clouds develop over the land and drift over the sea. Or Sc clouds tend to break to Cu as morning progresses. Or higher cloud sheet breaks up with morning leading to sunny periods when some Cu should appear	A sea breeze morning if wind less than 10–12 kt (moderate). See (50) for mode and times. Wind will slacken, possibly to calm if less than moderate. If more than moderate expect increase in speed, but some slackening is possible during the middle of the day. As off-shore wind early, slight seaway and expect what there is to slacken if sea breeze calms set in later in the period
Inshore zone with sea breeze or off-shore wind	1200– 1800 LST	Clear skies and sunshine if sea breeze blows. Cu may be visible inland. If no sea breeze, due to wind strength, then Cu cover at maximum and some sunny periods during afternoon. Good to excellent visibility unless industrial or other smoke sources ashore	If sea breeze has developed, expect steady on-shore breeze for the afternoon. Expect breeze to veer as afternoon progresses. Breeze will slacken towards end of period. Slight seaway at first but growing with duration of sea breeze. When sea breeze still developing in first part of period expect calms and fitful airs. Odd periods of wind from almost any direction. If wind speed has grown during the morning so that no sea breeze occurs, and no sign of sea breeze calms, then off-shore wind for rest of day. Small seaway because of short fetch
Inshore zone with calm or off-shore winds	1800– 0800 LST	Usually a clear evening. Cu over land may temporarily return to inshore zone but dies out with sunset. Often a clear night with risk of cloud again by dawn. Seaside town lights shining on cloud indicate change in the entirely fair situation. The cloud may be St (i.e. fog off the ground) that could mean fog on the sea later	Time of very little wind in fair conditions but nocturnal wind should aid passage making by midnight. Expect to lose nocturnal wind by dawn on many coasts. Sea should be slight, visibility good. Be suspicious of any new wind that springs up overnight from new quarter (other than off-shore)

Sailing Zones to Seaward of Main Coastline

The forecast will say something like: fair or fine with long sunny periods, winds light and variable, sea breezes around coasts. Average temperatures. Good visibility. Or: Mainly fair with sunny intervals. Risk of a shower during the afternoon. Wind light to moderate. Good visibility.
These two forecasts will cover most fair weather days, although wind strength may be higher.

In Southern Hemisphere for 'veer' read 'back' and vice versa.)

Wind quality	Expect	Variations for coastwise zone	Variations for offshore zone
Possibly random shifts at first. Becoming normal variability (68) with Cu development. Curious wide, indeterminate shifts as sea breeze develops late in period. If sea-breeze sets in then steady non-tactical airstream (64)	Sea breeze to continue if it has already set in unless an odd cloud bank, or shower cloud etc. comes along. If wind has calmed to fitful patches and Cu is not increasing, then sea breeze should start. If wind still from shore by end of period but slackening in speed, consider sea breeze during afternoon. If wind has increased to moderate or fresh then no sea breeze and present wind should continue	Look and feel of day as for Inshore zone. Sea breeze effects can reach limits of this zone when morning wind is very light. Can be late afternoon (if at all) when morning wind is moderate. Assess onset by calms as for Inshore. No true sea breeze? Can have shifts and lightening of the existing wind. Most other remarks as Inshore zone	Sea breeze only when morning wind is very light and clear with Cu ashore. Some shift or lightening in mid or late afternoon if wind less than 10 kt off-shore. Otherwise present wind to continue
If sea breeze has set in then steady non-tactical airstream. If sea breeze still developing (early part of period) then indeterminate shifts. If gradient wind continues from shorewards then normal and perhaps moderate (65) variability	Sea breeze to continue if it is already blowing but to veer and slacken perhaps to calm by end of period. Sea breeze that has produced calming over inshore waters can set in for a short while late in afternoon. Then return to off-shore wind. If all the sea breeze forces can do is reduce the speed of a moderate to fresh off-shore wind, then expect increase again with evening	Sea breeze usually does not show up in this zone until middle of period, so wait for signs of it. If clear skies above and Cu over land expect sea breeze effects to come. Early return to gradient wind farther from the shore. Some shift towards on-shore even in moderate to fresh coastwise directed winds. Most remarks for Inshore zone refer also to this zone, but sea breeze effects occur later farther from the shore	If sea breeze has not shown by 1600 then it probably will not. Possibly some shift to onshore in coastwise directed winds. Otherwise this zone unaffected by inshore forces
Evening shift patterns are often random although there can be moderate visibility. Overnight shift pattern is muted version of daytime one	Nocturnal wind by midnight if a clear night. If calm night then night wind will only be a few knots from shore. If wind already off-shore then nocturnal wind adds to off-shore gradient wind and can become moderate or more. Expect slackening of wind by dawn but some pick-up as sun rises appreciably	Calm evenings may see nocturnal wind reaching this zone. If gradient already returned to off-shore direction, expect increase with the night. Possibly more fitful gusts by dawn	Most unlikely to be any coastal influences

75

(Contd. over)

Fair Weather—Cumulus Clouds (Contd.)

Sailing venue	Time of day	Look and feel of the day	Sailing assesment
Inshore zone with on-shore winds	Dawn to dusk	Weather not of the land's making as in above. Therefore can be more cloudy by night than by day. If airstream cooler than the sea then Cu clouds, which may not survive ashore. If airstream warmer than sea then risk of sea fog and poor visibility (not truly applicable to this page) (84)	On-shore wind will only be assisted by sun on the land so expect wind increase with the day. Winds oblique to coastline. Can expect to shift with the day to more on-shore direction, but revert later to old direction or close to it. Seaway can be lumpy because of long fetch and day long duration of same or similar wind direction
Inshore zone with on-shore winds	Dusk to dawn	Usually no marked change in cloud type unless airstream is fed from a land mass not more than 50–100 miles away. Then some variation in cloud amount. Chance of showers during the night but not heavy ones	No great change during the night. Risk of more gusts by dawn than earlier in the night. If light at sunset then nocturnal wind influence can produce calm or fitful wind over inshore waters. Can reverse after midnight into off-shore drift. Otherwise on-shore for the night. (Unless gradient changes due to shifting pressure system) (24)

Sailing Zones to Seaward of Main Coastline (Contd.)

Wind quality	Expect	Variations for coastwise zone	Variations for offshore zone
Quality will depend on airstream and not on any other factor. So cannot make predictions about it when wind on-shore. Such wind may be gusty in the afternoon and will certainly become more turbulent with the day	Little change in type except for possible wind increase. Some change of direction near to the beach	Coastal effects will not extend this far out when wind is on-shore	No effects. Wind should be dictated by the pressure pattern, i.e. should be gradient wind
Wind quality is that of the sea. If air cooler than sea then normal, but low variability (65). If showery see (80). If no low cloud then variability might be anything. If air warmer than sea variability could be abnormal but also moderate or low in the scale	No great change with the night except for effects mentioned under Column 4	The effect of nocturnal wind influence against light on-shore evening winds is unlikely to extend very far into this zone	No effects that are worth mentioning

Overleaf:

Photo 15
A typical seascape of fair weather. The Inshore and Coastal waters are free of cloud, but Cu with perhaps an odd Cb (shower) cloud populate the seaward horizon. There is little or no upper cloud and the blue of the sea reflects the blue of the sky.

Photo 16
With no encumbrances to restrict the view, showers can be seen coming over the sea. Here the rain curtains below a shower cloud are easily seen. They mean strong gusty wind at the head of the shower and lighter wind behind it.

Big Cumulus, Cumulonimbus and Showers

A day of showers and bright periods with variable wind and squally gusts.
Main recognition points: Cool and clear early; rapidly developing Cu clouds that can grow to the dimensions of those in photo 17 with showers. Wind often north-westerly. Force 3–6.
Possible dangers: Moderate morning wind grows to fresh or even strong by afternoon. Intense gusts with showers. Occasional thunder.

Sailing venue	Time of day	Look and feel of day	Sailing assessment
Coastwise and Inshore with off-shore wind	Early forenoon 0800–0900 LST	Cool and clear early. Ragged Cu that develop early denote possible showers later. Often permanent windshifts when nocturnal wind influence wanes and later, when land inversion layer breaks. Good visibility for time of day	Variable wind from early morning, possibly widely variable. May already need to sit out and so expect hard sailing later. Consider shifts due to shoreside topography. Do cliffs extend wind shadow to your position? Shoreside refraction?
ditto	Forenoon 1000–1200	Day remains cool out of the sun. Cloud amount increasing in lower layers. Wind speed increasing	Often moderate wind so wind and sea will make for a wet sail in dinghies. The seaway may make it difficult to recognize considerable windshifts that can occur. Expect big gusts and perhaps a wetting as Cu clouds build into showers. Tactical advice: Tack in phase with the major windshifts obeying rules (68). If in doubt— do not tack. Do not try to cover your opponents
ditto	Afternoon 1300–1700	Often fresh with gusts to 25–30 kt. This is time of maximum wind speed but least variation in direction. However, showers will produce their own regime of variation. Some risk of isolated thunderstorms. Sometimes sea breeze affects lower inshore wind speed and so day feels warmer. If there were morning showers which have died out consider an airmass trough	Times of hardest sailing. Usually long dinghies will continually plane, short dinghies will frequently plane especially in gusts. There will be many capsizes in the gusty conditions. There will often be a seaway, and showers may bring heavy gusts cascading down off cliffs. Allow also for downdraught winds if there are showers over steeply sloping shores. (Particularly if showers tend to be thundery.) Entirely different conditions may obtain if morning wind has allowed sea breeze (90)
ditto	Evening 1800–Sunset	Coolish evening. Some lowering of visibility but no marked fall. Shower and other low clouds tend to reduce in size and form, Sc eventually dying out altogether. There can be Cu with silver linings against the setting sun	A calming of the wind and a steadying of the gust–lull sequence lead to more displacement sailing for dinghies. It is unusual to have good planing conditions in the evening. Tendency to establish abnormal wind shift pattern comes with establishment of inversion over the land

Sailing Zones to Seaward of main Coastline

Land Area Forecast will probably say something like: Fair or fine early, becoming showery later. Some showers may be heavy. In severe cases it may mention thunder although that does not mean a thunderstorm, just an occasional clap with a passing squally shower. Showers will die out overnight.
Sea Area Forecast: Can either mention continuous showers (no change with day or night) or no showers.

Wind quality	Diurnal variation	Expect	Remarks
Abnormal pattern possible at first reverting to normal gust cell pattern as sun stands higher	Time of lowest speed of the day but must increase	If wind already moderate then it will increase. If less than moderate consider sea breeze influence. Expect nearer gradient (forecast?) direction when sun breaks inversion over the land. (Recognized by appearance of Cu over the land)	This is the low speed time. If you do not like conditions now you will not be at all happy later
Early forenoon may be abnormally variable. Should become normally variable as Cu clouds build and develop into respectably-sized elements. Shower cells later	Time of increasing speed, lowered variability	Gradient wind to be established by this time. If wind more than moderate at beginning of period then little change in direction. If moderate or less expect some slackening and shift due to sea breeze. Inshore, wind can have extreme variability due to conflict between sea breeze and showers. If less than moderate (10 kt–8 kt) expect sea breeze to calm by afternoon. But showers can sweep away calms and re-establish gradient wind. Unusual to have 4–7 kt forenoon wind in these conditions, but if light, then anticipate sea breeze	This is the time of day and these are the zones where sea breeze influence will be most marked. A full sea breeze may not be established, but a sea breeze shift of some magnitude can occur
Gust cells with least directional variations but maximum speed variations. Shower cells with maximum intensity. Possibly reverting to abnormal pattern by end of period	Time of maximum wind speed. Time of maximum shower activity and strongest gusts. Time of minimum variation in direction, except when close to windward shores	Continuation of early afternoon conditions during the period up to 1700–1800 LST but shower frequency decreasing towards evening. Increasing direction variation towards end of period. As both sea breeze effect and strength of showers increase during this period to maximum and then die away together, there can be a conflict between them. The resulting extreme swings of direction and changes of speed are very marked. These days are, however, fortunately rare	The wind can be relied on to maintain its established pattern in the afternoon. There are exceptions but they are rare
Normal gust cells of afternoon tend to change to indeterminate shifts or abnormal pattern. Some tendency towards laminar flow	Time of strongest calming influences on the wind. Gust–lull sequence muted. Shower cells should have died out by end of period	Calming period to continue through the evening and after dusk, but if wind continues to blow from the land nocturnal wind will reinforce it. So expect increase of wind from the land with the night	This is a period when coastal waters are likely to have indeterminate shifts and very light periods

(Contd. over)

Sailing venue	Time of day	Look and feel of day	Sailing assessment
Coastwise and Inshore with off-shore wind	Night Sunset to Dawn	Clear skies, stars bright like jewels. Little seaway and a restful land wind without much variation. Later in night (towards dawn) possible showers develop over coastwise waters. Very often an increase in ragged Cu even if no showers develop	Very rarely a time for dinghies to be out. Coastal passage makers seek Inshore zone if prudent as maximum nocturnal wind found there. Wind should be perhaps Force 2–3 sometimes 4, but stronger night winds from the shore should be treated with suspicion. (Increasing gradient wind?) Carry less sail than by day to allow for occasional rogue gusts in nocturnal polar airstreams
Offshore or Coastwise with on-shore wind	Day or night	Much heap cloud with smaller ragged Cu between. Major passing showers. Cool, often blustery. Good to excellent visibility	Least wind behind showers, most under cloud leading edges and in precipitation
Inshore with on-shore wind	Forenoon and afternoon	Cool airstream with much heap cloud and occasional showers. Good visibility	Seaway at maximum for the conditions because of long sea fetch. Major cloud elements tell when shift pattern is imminent

Wind quality	Diurnal variation	Expect	Remarks
Light winds usually have random variability. If there is pattern it will be one of relatively short period	Sundown is time of low wind speed. Wind picks up with the night and often shifts direction. Falls again towards dawn	Few problems with nocturnal wind from the land, but allow for its loss later in the night. Possibility of showers over the coastal water by dawn. Some risk of strong katabatics where steep slopes come close to the sea	The night is a time when the polar air from the land should be benign
Normal gust cells between showers. Shower cells. Low variability outside showers	Not often noticeable. Possibly more showers by night	Little change in next few hours. Several shower cells. If showers cease: Barometer rising = fair, barometer steadying = immediately fair but possible deterioration later. Tomorrow, if showers continue: permanent veering shift. If showers cease rapidly: probably a back in advance of another low	Showers that are spaced in sequence fit tabulated conditions best. However, allow for airmass troughs where lines of showers come along preceded and followed by clear periods
Mainly random but shower cell pattern comes with bigger cloud elements	Little or none with fresh or stronger winds. When moderate or light, cloud tends to die out before reaching coast (if plenty of sunshine)	Morning wind to be shifted by sea breeze activity to more on-shore direction and reinforced in speed. If wind mainly parallel to the coastline then a cant shorewards often develops in the wind direction with the day. A reverse cant off the land develops with the night	The Inshore zone can modify even onshore winds, so allow for it doing so

Warm—perhaps Thundery Days

Main recognition points: Because temperate latitude sea temperature cannot be excessive, a hot or warm airstream must have an origin in the sub-tropics. Thus expect layers of cloud together with sunshine, poor visibility or sea fog. Thunderstorms formed over a land mass can move over the sea, but few storms originate over the water. Expect skies like (71) or (103).

Typical morning situation 0800–1000 LST	*Ways of recognizing change*	*Wind changes to expect*
Warm and humid. Poor visibility and often fog on coasts if not at sea. Wind from a warm quarter (usually a southern quadrant) which is typically moderate or less. Deck heads and deck hands may sweat	Signs of change are wrought in higher clouds. Clouds of the high or medium levels, (103) or (71) are examples, must move from hot land mass and obey the rule that they come from left hand of the surface wind direction, e.g. East coast of US: medium level clouds from W over warm southerly. English Channel: medium level clouds from S over warm easterly. Such orientations breed thunder. Be suspicious of backing and increasing wind in sultry conditions (Right hand of surface wind in Southern Hemisphere)	If it remains sunny, or if there are sunny periods over the land, allow for a sluggish sea breeze (Inshore and Coastwise but perhaps not the latter) that may not start until afternoon. If thundery-type cloud thickens then surface wind will usually increase and perhaps back a little. When thunder heard, storms within ten miles. When sky like photo 17, then allow immediately for gusts to 30–40 knots (possibly more) torrential rain and hail etc. Storms ashore draw in air from seaward + sea breeze? = moderate or more, on-shore wind. Most intense storms move up against a wind they are sucking into themselves. So wind that sluggishly shifts towards coming bad storm means intense thunder squalls later *from* the direction of storm

Typical early night situation. Dusk to midnight	*Ways of recognizing change*	*Wind changes to expect*
Depends on events of the day. 1. No storms and no sea breeze: probably remaining warm and humid, and keeping gradient wind. 2. Visibility still poor: St cloud may form over coasts which sometimes drifts over adjacent sea. Always risk of fog—avoid shipping lanes. 3. Sea breeze by day (Inshore and Coastwise, or maybe only the former): evening coastal calms or very light wind from any quarter not off-shore, can become nocturnal wind. 4. Storms that have now stopped or receded: cooler, gradient that may be locally bent by storms. Often considerable cloud in medium and high layers. However, St is possible as a formless sheet of foggy cloud, possibly only a few hundred feet off the deck	Difficult to recognize signs of change at night. Remarks above apply to night as well as day but coastal thunderstorms are usually phenomena that die with the night. Lightning and thunder heard: storms within 10 miles. 'Summer lightning' (no thunder heard) storms more than 10 miles away. Storms come from direction in which medium level clouds move. (As, Ac drifting across moon?) Over adjacent coast? Could well die over sea unless upper storms. (Lots of cloud top lightning strokes.) Nocturnal wind can generate coastal showers and storms late in the night with attendant gusts	If light evening wind (or calm) then nocturnal wind, but not if St forms over the land (watch for coastal town lights loomed on low clouds). However, wind after inland storms often comes from shorewards and may look like nocturnal wind. Consider return to gradient direction (forecast?) later in night. If storms persist over local sea area consider wind changes as above

Sailing Zones to Seaward of Main Coastline

The forecast will probably say something like: Mainly fair, thunderstorms (or risk of them) later (usually afternoon or evening), visibility poor, sea fog. Wind light to moderate at first, becoming fresh for a time later.

Expect later	Remarks
If no storms develop, existing gradient wind should continue into evening and night. If no storms, and a seabreeze develops then expect light evening inshore wind or even calm, when visibility will be very poor. If storms ride in across the surface wind direction, after they have passed expect wind from direction they came. If intense storm comes towards its wind, expect light to moderate wind in rear, to come from left of line of advance of storm. Very sluggish nocturnal wind in light, fair, night conditions	Storms are of two kinds. Surface storms bend surface wind to themselves and they are the ones that move towards their own wind. Upper storms are the ones which occur along fronts and which usually move across the surface wind. Later such storms may descend to near the surface. Waterspouts occur in association with intense thundery activity as do tornado storm spouts, but where and when they occur cannot be predicted. They are more likely off Florida and the Gulf States than farther north. Waterspouts are mainly whirlwinds of vapour but tornado spouts could swamp a cockpit, even if the intense winds—up to 200 kt—could be countered. Luckily it is very rare for a yacht to meet such conditions. Hurricanes are not included here. Unnatural warmth and skies that look thundery precede them, but only the hurricanes warning service can give precise information. In any case hurricanes and yachts do not mix
Passage of a thundery trough leaves a new wind situation. Expect tomorrow's wind to be veered on today's when upper storms pass. Can still be warm with low visibility. Surface storms produce new cooler conditions tomorrow (forecast?). If cooler airstream, then probably a cumulus day (74) with gradient from a direction veered to today's direction	The wind tomorrow can hardly be the same as today if thunderstorms occur widely. Upper storms are formed on warm fronts and winds veer when they pass. Surface storms that form in lines across the wind are usually on cold fronts and winds again veer when they pass. A thundery occluded front can have appearance of both kinds without respite. Tomorrow must then be cooler with probably a return to good visibility and fleets of Cu. Persistent warm days without storms do occur and then gradient wind can be modified by nocturnal wind at night unless gradient too strong. No storms despite heat, means anticyclonic tendency

Photo 17 *(p. 86)*
The threatening and chaotic sky that runs just ahead of a very intense thundery trough. This one capsized most of the dinghies racing around the coast of south-east England one Sunday afternoon. The initial gust was estimated to be about 50 knots.

Increasing High Cloud and Backing Winds

Photo 18 *(p. 87)*
That conditions will deteriorate pre-supposes that they are now fair. Here the signs of approaching trouble are written in the Ci aloft. The main elements are more or less in line. If they stay like that but increase while the wind shows signs of backing, then expect poorer weather.

Main recognition points: Mainly fair, anticyclonic weather now and in immediate past. Upper sky beginning to cloud over—usually from a westerly point. Wind showing signs of backing towards a more southerly point. Possible dangers: Increasing wind in the next 6–12 hours—possibly a sharp blow. Chance of squalls later and bad weather generally.

Sailing venue	Previous history	Weather now	Sailing assessment
Main coastline facing S or SE. Wind now SW to NW	A period of fair weather with Cu clouds by day and clear skies at night. Not much high cloud before, but more has encroached in recent past. Wind typically W or NW moderate, or often less. Has begun to back towards SW or S or shows tendency to do so	Ci invading upper sky. Cu, if any, beginning to shred and die out. Often very good or exceptional visibility. Wind should have backed somewhat, perhaps now SW to S and some signs of increasing speed	Easy conditions now, with a small seaway due to land fetch, can change to difficult conditions with growing seaway as wind develops sea fetch and increases. (Wave height estimate from page 20)
Same as above but coast faces E or NE	As above	As above	Unless wind backs to SE (east-facing coast), waters will be sheltered and above remarks about land fetch apply. If wind does back off the sea then above remarks on sea fetch apply to E coast
Same as above but coast faces W or SW	As above	As above	Present onshore wind (often with Cu clouds and sometimes with showers) will remain onshore as wind backs, so expect sea conditions to become more lumpy. Allow for cross sea as new wind direction generates waves
Same as above but coast faces NW to W	As above	As above	Onshore wind (if any) will soon go offshore and may temporarily fall lighter. Present seaway will be replaced by less lumpy one and it can be quite smooth inshore at first

Forecast will probably say something like: Mainly fair at first but becoming cloudy later. Rain probably spreading during the outlook period. Winds will be light to moderate at first but will back southerly later and increase to fresh. (This page only refers to changes in the period when the sky is first clouding over. See (30) and (36) for later.)

Wind quality	Diurnal variation	Expect	Tomorrow	Remarks
Moderate, usually normal variability at first under Cu. Becoming rather random as upper cloud cuts off sun's heat. However, may still have considerable shifts in it. As wind swings from off the sea any normal variability will be lower in the scale. Yet increasing wind will bring larger, random, turbulent eddies	As (42–45) when wind off the land. No noticeable variation when wind comes off the sea. (Unless another coast is not more than 50 miles distant)	More cloud. Frontal weather. Wind to increase from southerly direction. Rain later. (See (24) and (30) for details of shifts that come with lows and fronts)	Only the forecast can help here. The most likely event is showers but it could be foggy, or low cloud and muggy warmth. It depends how fast the weather moves	If clouds increase but wind stays doggedly where it is, then usually not much change
Under influence of land, winds should remain variable but become more random in shift pattern as the sky clouds over	Usual variation when day only partly cloudy but this can be over-ridden by winds of the low	As above	As above	
Normal variability if Cu or Cb off the sea. Random turbulence of fairly low variability if wind off the sea, under full cloud cover and with increasing wind. If abnormal variability (64) (and this applies to above cases as well) then allow for a thundery trough or gusty heavy showers later	Should be little or none	As above	As above	
Often Cu or Cb off the sea at first, so normal variability. As wind backs Cu will die out and shift pattern will become indeterminate	Daytime turbulence and convection currents when the wind comes off the land. If shift spans the evening period then wind will be very slow to pick up and can be quite light at first	As above	As above, but if warm air tomorrow then wind will probably be off the land or parallel to it. If showers, today's wind pattern can be repeated, although probably more virile than today	

Fair Weather—Cumulus Clouds

Photo 19 *(p. 94)*
When you sail on lakes, rivers, etc., inland from the coast you can see the sea breeze front coming, as in this photo which is taken some 15 miles inland. The sea is beyond the ridge of the coastal hills and there is not much cloud anywhere except for the cloud line that is the sea breeze front. A similar line very often exists to warn that a sea breeze shift is coming.

Main recognition points: Clear early with normal or below average temperatures for the time of year. Often a sunny and bright morning with little low cloud. What there is may be mist patches lifting out of hollows etc. Any higher cloud is usually thin and well broken. Cu clouds develop in the forenoon but not too early, i.e. after 0800–0900 LST. Early and rapid development—photo 19. Visibility—good.

Sailing venue	Time of day	Look and feel of the day	Sailing assessment
Beachland zone with off-shore wind. Coastal zone variations in Column 7 Inland zone variations in Column 8	0800–1200 LST	Early: Clear and often cool. Good visibility. Occasional mist patches that quickly clear. Later: Cu clouds develop—first over slopes in the sun. May remain individual on best days, or flatten and spread into Sc layer. This layer often thins later. High cloud sheets tend to break as morning progresses	A sea breeze morning if wind less than 4–6 kt at about 0800–0900 LST. See (50–57) for mode and times. Expect wind to slacken—calm patches by mid-morning ahead of sea breeze shift. If wind 5–9 kt (0800–0900 LST) a sea breeze afternoon. Wind shift or wind 10–15 kt: sea breeze slackening the gradient wind around middle of the day is only likely possibility (except lower latitudes). More than 15 kt no great change with the day. An interesting sailing morning with great tactical possibilities
Beachland zone with sea breeze or off-shore wind	1200–1800 LST	If sea breeze blows then usually clear skies to seaward of sea breeze front. Cooling, steady sea wind. If sea breeze front in vicinity then heavy Cu clouds and odd wind shifts. Local haze. If moderate or more off-shore wind then usually Cu fleets or Sc layer and warm. Moderate visibility	If sea breeze has developed, then steady, but often slowly veering wind for the afternoon. Tendency to slacken towards coastal calms by end of period. Morning wind of 5–9 kt often yields afternoon to onset of sea breeze. Short duration with possibility of return to off-shore wind at first sign of sea breeze slackening. Odd wind shifts before onset. Moderate to fresh off-shore wind may be shifted if good day, but no true sea breeze
Beachland zone with light winds or calm or off-shore wind	1800–0800 LST	Usually a clear if hazy evening. Any low cloud dies out with evening. Often a clear night with bright stars. Any low cloud at evening or early night may mean trouble	After sea breeze day, evening is typically calm, or light winds. Nocturnal wind is likely by midnight (58). Gradient wind (above sea breeze by day) may come from new quarter at evening and be the wind for the night. A depression encroaching? See (24) and (116

The forecast will say something like: Fair or fine with long sunny periods, winds light and variable, sea breezes around coasts. Average temperatures.
Or: Mainly fair with sunny intervals. Risk of a shower during the afternoon. Wind light to moderate or moderate to fresh. It may mention lifted fog patches in the morning. Otherwise good visibility.

Wind quality	Expect	Variations for Coastal	Variations for Inland
Early: Often random shifts. When Cu develop: normal shift pattern (68). Before sea breeze front arrives often abnormal for a time (72). Wide shifts in vicinity of the front but can pass rapidly and wind from landward suddenly becomes wind from seaward (46–51). Sea breeze current is usually non-tactical. If moderate to fresh Cu airstream: normal variability	Sea breeze to continue if it has already set in unless some odd-looking cloud banks, showers, overcast come along. If wind still off-shore by end of period, but slackening in speed— sea breeze imminent? If wind still off-shore by end of period but increasing, then not much chance of the breeze. However, maximum sea breeze force middle of afternoon, so possibly some shift later	Sea breeze frequently does not reach this zone before 1200. So often morning of mixed normal and abnormal wind patterns that shows slight tendency to increase. Expect afternoon sea breeze, especially beyond a range of coastal hills. If wind greater than 10–15 kt and no depth in the Cu then probably no breeze	As Coastal, but sea breeze effects come correspondingly later, if at all. Therefore unlikely to have sea wind in this zone in this period
Normal: When Cu and off-shore wind persist. Abnormal: When late sea breeze front hovers. Odd shifts: When sea breeze front virtually overhead, calms and fitful shifts. Non-tactical sea breeze current when latter established	Early part of period: If no sea breeze yet but other conditions are right, look for sea breeze front (53). Sea breeze front middle of afternoon leads to odd calms and curious shifts Beachland and nearer Coastal zones. If moderate–fresh then expect diurnal loss of speed with evening. There is often a shift of direction at this time	Time for sea breeze to invade coastal region and blow through it in early period. Times etc. (53). When morning wind 6–8 kt sea breeze front can hover in this zone	Time for sea breeze to appear Inland. Times etc. (53). When morning wind 6–8 kt sea breeze front can hover in this zone. Only best sea breeze days find front 30–40 miles inland by end of period
Sea breeze non-tactical stream falters and dies. Odd shifts as evening wind takes over but then indeterminate shift pattern. Nocturnal wind will be steady and surface hugging. Shoreside shift pattern dictated by topography	Light airs evening following sea breeze day. Increase in high cloud with filaments in many directions means fair weather tomorrow. Filaments and banners in one direction means likely deterioration (30) and (36)	Sea breeze can continue to blow lightly until dusk. If not, almost or total calm. If sea breeze swept away by another wind, that is often the wind for the night	Best sea breeze days find front advancing inland until about 2100–2200 LST. Evening calms. Nocturnal wind usually only in seaward side of this zone

91

(Contd. over)

Fair Weather—Cumulus Clouds (Contd.)

Sailing venue	Time of day	Look and feel of the day	Sailing assessment
Beachland zone with on-shore winds	Dawn to dusk	Cool morning early and often ragged sea Cu that becomes Sc over land. If cloud cover early allow for its breaking later with sun's heat. If clear early, sun's heat can generate cloud later	Early morning wind is gradient (cannot be nocturnal wind because of direction). If broken skies then sea breeze forces add to wind strength. Strongest mid-afternoon, lessening with evening. Wind direction can be shifted by effect of strong sea breeze to be more directly on-shore. Allow for a gusty blow in afternoon if early wind is gentle to moderate. If more, consider safety later in day
Beachland zone with on-shore winds	Dusk to dawn	Cloud from the sea at dusk likely to remain for night. However, the airstream should either be Cu from the sea or clear. If nocturnal wind blows then usually clear of low cloud over land, but much ragged Cu or Cb over Inshore and Coastwise zones	Wind from the sea at night can have entirely different feel to wind off the land at night. It is more like daytime wind. Allow for gusts and eddies. If above 7–10 kt little reason for this wind to change. However, nocturnal wind effect can reduce or reverse light on-shore night winds. Calms between phases of the shifts

Wind quality	Expect	Variations for Coastal	Variations for Inland
Quality in this zone is dependent on the nature of the airstream and not on the land mass. However, there will be normal variability with Cu airstreams from the sea, but land heating produces gusts and turbulent eddies and these may appear random in time	Often little change in wind type except for diurnal variation. Approaching night should have similar wind direction. However, consult forecast for likely changes	Remarks in Column 4 apply to Coastal zone as well as Beachland	Little useful can be said
Nocturnal wind from the sea can have normal variability made more noticeable by being largely devoid of turbulent eddies	Light evening on-shore wind can be nullified by nocturnal wind, but allow for return to on-shore by dawn	Similar remarks to Beachland zone	Little useful can be said

Big Cumulus, Cumulonimbus and Showers

Photo 20 *(p. 95)*
A great shower cloud sweeps in across an estuary. The rain curtains (where the cloud seems to be joined to the ground) are the scene of very strong gusts, while lesser gusts will occur under the out-riding clouds. The latter are lifted on the outflowing cold air around the main shower centre.

A day of showers and bright periods with variable wind and squally gusts. Main recognition points: Cool and clear early; rapidly developing Cu that can grow to the proportions shown in photo 20 by late morning or afternoon with showers. Typical wind direction NW Force 3–5.
Possible dangers: Mean wind speed doubles in heavier gusts especially when associated with showers. Many capsizes on sheltered waters as gusts ignore shoreside hamper. Occasional thunder.

Sailing venue	Time of day	Look and feel of the day	Sailing assessment
Beachland and Coastal with off-shore wind. *Note.* Apart from sea breeze effects, most of the information applies also to inland venues	Early forenoon 0800–0900 LST	Cool and clear early. However, some mist pockets may exist and have to clear as foggy cloud that converts to Cu. Ragged Cu early denotes showers later. Early morning wind often seems quite strong for the time of day. Usually good visibility. Not much high cloud	Variable wind from early morning. Anticipate permanent wind shifts: 1. When overnight off-shore wind influence wanes. 2. When sun breaks the overnight inversion layer. 3. When sea breeze influence increases. If you have to sit out a dinghy at this time you will be fighting the gusts later. Consider shoreside shifts (60)
As above	Forenoon 1100–1200	Day warms up in the sun, but remains cool in the shade. Cu cloud cover increases but should remain broken for showers to follow. If Cu spreads to cover whole sky then no showers and diminished gusts	Wind that increases to moderate by this time will lead to good planing conditions and may be too strong for dinghies by afternoon. Can expect to get wet both from the sky and over the bow. If showers occur then allow for big gusts as they strike. If wind less than moderate, anticipate sea breeze slowing the wind and perhaps a marked sea breeze shift (52). Showers will sweep away such influences
As above	Afternoon 1300–1700	Showery airstreams usually make Force 4–5 by afternoon. There should be blue breaks between showers. However, minor troughs produce extended showers sometimes preceded and succeeded by clearer weather. Risk of thunderstorms but these should be isolated and passing. If not, see (100)	Often tough sailing. Gusts at maximum but possibly not as noticeable as morning gusts because afternoon mean speed higher. Expect a capsize in dinghies. Allow for wind increase (17) on leaving harbour for outside. Days when showers die out early, or form late, can allow sea breeze effects in Beachland if not Coastal zone (90)

...and area forecast will probably be something like: Fair or fine becoming showery later. Showers may be heavy (in severe ...ases they can mention risk of thunder). Showers will die out overnight. (Excludes coasts with on-shore winds where showers can ...ontinue throughout the night.) Despite forecast, if no showers materialize in your area then reason can be that you lie in a ...hower shadow (in lee of hills on which air sheds its shower potential) or the air aloft subsides as a whole and prevents the ...howers building. Latter may mean rain later if cloud increases aloft, or fair weather if upper sky remains mainly blue.

Wind quality	Expect	Remarks
Abnormal pattern (72) possible at first ...everting to normal pattern (68) as sun ...ises higher. For variation with time of ...ay see Diurnal variation column (81)	Wind strength to increase. Increase usually marked when Cu forms. However, it may not have formed at this early time. When Cu forms expect wind to shift closer to gradient (forecast?) direction	This is the characteristic weather immediately behind a depression that has just passed. It may go on for days or revert quickly to fair (with risk of another depression)
...an still be abnormal if sun has not ...roken overnight inversion layer. ...owever, this airstream will have ...ormal variability on most occasions. ...ormal pattern (68) as soon as Cu ...louds develop	Gradient wind to become established during the early part of this period. Formation of Cu shows convection currents that bring the gradient wind to the surface. Bright mornings without too much Cu or Cb cloud can induce sea breeze-slackening of wind near the coastline. Must always allow for sea breeze to assert if wind allows (52). If wind is 8–10 kt or less from the land, sea breeze can occur over Beachland, but any showers will normally re-establish gradient wind	If the airstream that ought to be showery (your own or someone else's forecast) is not and there are no signs of large Cb clouds, and if wind less than 10 kt, see (74). If more, this page is best
...nder Cu: Gust cells with least ...irection variations but maximum speed ...ariations. Under Cb (showers): ...hower cells (64) with maximum ...ntensity. Spring and Fall: Expect a ...eturn to abnormal variability by end of ...eriod	Continuation of early afternoon conditions with wind increase to maximum at mid-afternoon. Then a general slow decrease in speed with a marked slowing by end of period. If wind does not fall with onset of evening then expect increasing gradient wind. Why? Barometer falling? (88). Wind shift by, or around, end of period as Cu or Cb clouds die out can be back or veer. If wind not fresh, and showers or large Cu over Beachland, then anticipate sea breeze effects under best conditions (53)	Beachland and seaward side of Coastal zones are liable to have sea breeze shifts in this period even though conditions seem to be biased against them

97

(Contd. over)

Big Cumulus, Cumulonimbus and Showers (Contd.)

Sailing venue	Time of day	Look and feel of the day	Sailing assessment
Beachland and Coastal with off-shore wind	Evening 1800–sunset	Showers die out but thunderstorms can continue. Usually clearing skies. Wind speed dies down rapidly. Gusts die. Some fall of visibility but not marked	Calming of the wind and a muted gust–lull sequence produces more displacement sailing. Wind can fall very dramatically in speed and shift direction somewhat. If showery morning and sea breeze afternoon, anticipate evening calm on sheltered waterways
As above	Night Sunset to dawn	Clear skies. Bright stars. Cool night especially on the water	Evening wind will normally continue through the night if speed above 8–10 kt. If less expect nocturnal wind to add to it. If calm after sunset allow for nocturnal wind (58). Leaving harbour with gentle to moderate wind allow for increase when clear of land (17)
Beachland and Coastal with on-shore wind	Forenoon and Afternoon	Airstream must be cooler than the sea for showers to form. Thus seaborne showers most likely in Beachland zone on coasts with a northerly aspect. In Coastal and Inland zones showers can form over the land even though none over the sea. Visibility good apart from showers	There are many possibilities. Wet, cool showery air off the sea is uncomfortable sailing weather. Steep short sea when tide ebbs in estuaries etc. Usually a lot of cloud whose amount varies only with state of the airstream and nothing else. Farther inland on rivers, reservoirs etc. gusty showers or much Cu with moderate variability (108)
As above	Evening and Night	No diurnal variation in onshore showery airstreams, so showers continue through the night. Generally cool and wind does not appreciably decrease in evening. Showers may even enhance over Beachlands before dawn. Farther inland ragged Cu but showers may die out	Allow for sometimes invisible showers and their gusts (19). No showers now does not mean that the night will be wholly free of them. If leaving sheltered harbour or estuary allow for wind increase and gusts (17)

Wind quality	Expect	Remarks
Normal gust cells of afternoon tend to change to indeterminate or abnormal shift pattern. Tendency to laminar flow in creeks with extensive mudflats at low water	This is the period when the wind mutes most strongly. Fall in speed with clear skies may be enough to make later increase due to nocturnal wind effects quite evident. However, such effects occur in next period unless strong katabatics from shoreside slopes are present	There ought to be gradient wind from the land during this period but sometimes there are calms or indeterminate shifts in these zones
Light winds will have indeterminate variability. Stronger winds can carry on an undulating gust–lull pattern	If gradient has continued from land in previous period expect wind to continue for most of the night. Greatest chance of no wind is about dawn. Allow for katabatics from local slopes close to the coastline	Moonlight sailing is not usual for dinghies, but cruisers may need this night information
Gusty shifts are going to be normal, but variability will be fairly low. Showers enhance gust speeds but should bring veered direction in Northern Hemisphere (backed in Southern Hemisphere). Low wind speed can bring long periods of confused showery shifts	Showers to continue through the day, but if they do not, look for signs of developing higher clouds—depression encroaching? Other possibilities include the subsiding air in developing anticyclonic weather that damps out showers. Upper sky should be losing cloud in this case. Low wind speed (6–12 kt) and coastal hills can induce big showers and sometimes thunderstorms. Allow for more on-shore direction shift on days when sea breeze influences are strong. Also allow for sea breeze adding to wind speed in middle of the day	The on-shore wind is governed by both the sea temperature and the air temperature. Many on-shore weather regimes are possible, e.g. Clear over the sea—cloud builds over the land. Sea breeze effects can make coastal belts cloud free even with on-shore winds
For night period variability is relatively high and gusts associated with showers (and sometimes even without showers) continue. However, nocturnal wind influences act against the on-shore wind, so allow for reduced speed and more stable conditions after midnight	Showers in the evening to continue through the night, possibly with breaks but enhanced at times. With evening, Force 4 or less wind slackens in middle of night. Possible pick up by morning but farther inland wind will have night time lulling usually experienced overland	On-shore night winds can produce many different effects over the land. Only a few can be covered and here we have concentrated on the airstream which develops showers over the sea and sweeps them inland

Main recognition points: History of heat and perhaps an extended spell of fine weather that has now grown overhot and humid. Much more cloud aloft than hitherto. Poorish visibility—heat haze. Wind may come from an unusual quarter, e.g. E when prevailing winds are westerly or from some other quarter, such as S or SW when weather oppressive.

Typical morning situation 0800–1200 LST	Ways of recognizing change	Wind changes to expect
Warm or close, often with little wind at first. Cloud like (71) drifting in on high or medium level winds. Usually not much low cloud in early part of day. Hazy or poor visibility. There may be fog on the coast itself	If upper cloud moves from left* of gradient wind, anticipate thundery rain or thunderstorms by late afternoon—if not before. A likely pattern is that medium level cloud will diminish during the middle of the day and then new forms will increase to wholly overcast. At first probably like photo 21. Allow for the surface wind being sea breeze, when the rule above will not apply. Ask a weather office what the gradient direction might be and at the same time ask them what they think it will do *'Right' in Southern Hemisphere.	Sea breeze? (52) and (53). If moderate or fresh expect gradient to persist with some backing. If wind backs as cloud increases expect deterioration. Wind increasing into the afternoon. If thundery rain or thunderstorms arrive expect intermittent gusts. Gusts can become very strong (30–50 kt) when sky grows to look like (86). When storm line passes expect cooler, moderate or fresh wind from direction in which medium clouds were drifting this morning
As above	If gradient wind blows more or less parallel to direction in which upper cloud moves (the cloud form (62) tends to set in lines along the wind at its level) then, although there may be changes in the amount of cloud, no great weather changes should occur (Applies to Southern Hemisphere without change)	More chance of sea breeze as cloud tends to decrease in this situation. When wind moderate or fresh expect persistence of morning pattern through the day. However, note that should the surface wind back,* it can bring the above deteriorating situation. * 'Veer' in Southern Hemisphere
History of frontal cloud that is now breaking and decreasing. Now somewhat cooler than of late. Sky may resemble (35). The remarks apply when this clearance occurs at any time of the forenoon or early afternoon	If upper cloud comes from the right* of the gradient wind direction, cloudiness, now aloft, should decrease. Cu clouds should develop but remain relatively small. Like (63) at first, becoming (55) later *'Left' in Southern Hemisphere	Sea breeze is more probable as both sunshine and Cu development aid sea breeze. If moderate or fresh, wind should have veered* or be veering soon to a new permanent direction. Speed will increase with the day *'Backed' in Southern Hemisphere

Wind quality	Remarks
Usually abnormal and sometimes highly variable (72) particularly when light. Random in fog or when fog is lifting into rather formless masses of low cloud. Tending to become normally variable if Cu develops (68)	These days do not necessarily result in thunder but they often presage a breakdown in present fine spell. The situation depicted is that of an encroaching front which has been forced into being thundery by surface heating. Thus it is most likely to occur in summer when fronts approach over a heated land mass
Often abnormal with moderate variability. Very often becoming normal with afternoon. Cu cloud development is accompanied by a change to normal shift pattern	The morning may look and feel just like the above but nothing much happens, because the upper and surface winds need to be transposed before change is indicated
Possibly random now but can be normal or abnormal at this early hour. Most likely to become normal by afternoon if Cu develop. Cu does not have to develop however in very dry airstreams	This is a situation where it is envisaged that an old cold front or occlusion is passing. When the sky is observed after the front has just passed, it will not often look like the text books. There is often very little cloud at low levels and that above is broken up. However, some connected linear features may still exist in the cloud aligned across the wind. Whether cloudy or not there is nearly always a veer* of wind when the front passes

*'Back' in Southern Hemisphere

101

(Contd. pp. 104, 105)

Photo 21 *(opposite)*
Calm now, but the multi-layers of cloud moving in, coupled to the sultry quiet, make it worth considering if this cloud layer does not herald trouble in the shape of massive thunderstorms later.

Typical afternoon situation 1300–1500 LST	Ways of recognizing change	Wind changes to expect
Morning was warm but there is now increasing high cloud. Any morning fog has lifted but visibility is still not very good	Very definite thundery looking sky encroaching overhead from left* of morning wind i.e. the wind before the sea breeze— if any. Expect thunderstorms or thundery rain *'Right' in Southern Hemisphere	Present wind regime should be invaded by new forces. If storms are coming then increasing tendency for wind to go towards storms when less than 10 kt already. If 15–20 kt or more expect to remain more or less in present direction followed by a sudden, savage, takeover by storm winds when they threaten overhead. Great cold gusts from direction of the nearer storm centre
Cloudless afternoon with a cooling sea breeze. Some upper cloud perhaps, but not at all threatening as was the previous situation	If Beachland or Coastal, look inland for sight of storms developing over hills. Sea breeze feeds such storms. The downdraught winds sweep away the sea breeze	Continuing sea breeze now, but if storms develop, downdraught winds from inland will sweep sea breeze into the sea by, or during, the evening. Then cold wind from the land, perhaps for rest of the night. If thunder heard, possible strong wind from that direction soon

Sailing Zones to Landward of Main Coastline (Contd.)

Wind quality	Remarks
Because of convection currents, afternoon winds are far more likely to be normal than abnormal. However, if day is very hot and still no sea breeze develops then abnormal pattern can persist. If sea breeze has set in, present random or other shift pattern will be replaced by the regime of the storms, should they develop	The hot, hazy morning may have foretold thunder, but nothing happened. It is far more likely to occur as the day wears on
Sea breeze means random non-tactical shifts, but near to developing stormline expect strange shifts with tendency at first to blow towards storms and then later from them	The sea breeze that develops on these hot humid days is often sluggish. It may be slow to develop, slow to move inland and even then only blow gently. However, if storms develop on inland hill ridges these can give the sea breeze a sudden jerk in the afternoon or early evening

Photo 22 *(opposite)*
Sometimes the wind can get very strong even under blue skies. This can happen on the edges of anticyclones when depressions are trying to muscle in.

Because there are so many possibilities, a hypothetical lake (Fig. 6) (47) has been chosen to illustrate the different winds that can be encountered. It is assumed to have high ground on three sides and the open southerly aspect is representative of waters which debouch on to plains. Effects characteristic of lakes with rising ground on one side only are also covered. The reader can rotate the diagram if the open aspect of a lake does not lie to the S. When high ground exists close to only one side of the body of water, read the lower sections below.

Aspect	Thermal tendencies (quiet weather)
Rising ground on three sides as Fig. 6 (wooded slopes to the water's edge may preclude anabatics)	*Morning* Anabatic drift to W shore and later to N. *Afternoon* Daily increase in gradient wind usually over-rides most thermal influences, but N winds lowered in speed and S winds enhanced. E and W winds tend towards N. *Evening* Katabatic drift from W shore
Rising ground mainly to W	*Morning* Maximum tendency to anabatic drift to W shore. *Afternoon* Waning anabatic influence on W shore. Gradient winds from N or S quadrants steered more parallel to W shore when high ground not far distant. *Evening* Early katabatic tendency for drift off W shore
Rising ground mainly to N	*Morning* Maximum tendency to anabatic drift to N shore late in the morning and continuing into the afternoon. *Afternoon* Waning anabatic influence on N shore as afternoon progresses. Steering of winds from W or E quadrants. *Evening* Katabatic drift from N shore
Rising ground mainly to E	*Morning* Little thermal influence in the earlier part of the forenoon. *Afternoon* Some increasing anabatic drift to E shore. Steering of winds from N and S quadrants along E shore. *Evening* Maximum anabatic tendency, but this is small compared to tendency when rising ground is to W or N
Rising ground mainly to S	Little or no anabatic tendencies in morning or afternoon. However slight slopes can catch sur and provide some drift to S. Equally little katabatic drift in evening and night. Allow for steering of existing wind

Tactical rule If beating into a wind with a topographic or thermal cant in it, tack towards the side that the wind cants. Example: In Fig. 6 (47) tacking up the W shore towards mark M, assume gradient wind has N tendency but tends to be NW rather than NE. Wind funnels through (D) and fans. Tack towards (D) (starboard tack) and get a favourable lift for the mark. Wind will come progressively more from port of the mark so tack that way. Other examples would follow same principle.

Topographic steering (Gentle, moderate or possibly strong gradient winds)	*Funnelling and fanning (Gradient winds, strength above gentle)*
N winds tend to become NW or SW over lake. Wind shadow possible off W shore. *N winds* tend to become NW or NE. Wind shadow possible off N shore. *E winds* tend to become NE or SE. Wind shadow possible over NE part of lake. *S winds* tend to become SE or SW in extreme S corners (A) and (B)	*NW winds* funnel and fan into W along N shore and N along W shore. Holes may appear in the wind in the centre of lake. *NE winds* funnel and fan into E along N shore and N along E and W shores (remember to add thermal tendencies). *SE winds* preserve form until forced to funnel on NW shore. *SW winds* steered into S on W shore. *S winds* must split to funnel out NE and NW and there can be a hole off N shore. Wind increase at (C) and (D)
W winds tend to become NW in (D) and SW in (A). *N winds* locally enhance speed along W shore and over centre of lake generally. *E winds* split over central W side of lake. *S winds* steer and increase speed on W shore also over centre of lake	*NW winds* enhance in (D); fan into N wind towards (A). Tend to W in (B). *NE winds* fan into E in (D) and fan into N along W shore. *SE winds* steer from S on W shore. *SW winds* fan into S along W shore
W winds steer and enhance on N shore. Local increase over centre of lake. *N winds* are steered into NW at (D) and NE at (C). *E winds* steer like W winds. *S winds* tend to split into (D) and (C)	*NW winds* fan into W winds over (C). *NE winds* fan into E winds over (D). *SE winds* steer into E winds along N shore. *SW winds* steer into W winds along N shore
N winds split into (C) and (B). *N winds* steer on E shore and enhance over lake centre. *E winds* tend to be NE in (C) and SE in (B). *S winds* would in case shown, tend to take a curved path from (B) to (C) with locally enhanced speed over centre of lake	*NW winds* funnel into (B). *NE winds* steer into N winds along E shore. *SE winds* funnel out of (B) and fan towards (C) and (D). *SW winds* steer into S winds along E shore or turn into W winds in (B)
N winds tend to steer along S shore and enhance in speed in (B). *N winds* tend to split into (A) and (B). *E winds* would fan out of (B) and steer into (A). *S winds* would tend to come from SW or SE in (A) or (B) but enhance in speed over central and N part of lake	*NW winds* steer towards W winds along S shore. *NE winds* steer towards E winds along S shore. *SE winds* steer into E winds along S shore. *SW winds* steer into W winds along S shore

Mountain Lakes, Tarns etc.

Photo 23 *(p. 114)*
Lake sailing when mountains or any high land come close to the water's edge can be hazardous for the unprepared. Here on the Wolfgansee in Austria we are looking at a situation where mountain and valley winds will dominate when the weather overall is quiet.

The hypothetical site chosen is typical of mountain lakes that tend to be long and narrow (finger or moraine-dammed lakes) and very deep in places. The end of the lake often debouches into an alluvial plain and then looks up a valley to mountains. The thermal and topographic wind regimes of such lakes differ depending on which direction they point (Fig. 7) (49).

Valley C looks	Morning regime	Early afternoon	Late afternoon	Evening
North	Anabatic drift up slopes (A). Developing tendency for drift up (B). Slack tendency towards (C). Cu clouds mainly over (A)	Equal tendencies to anabatic drift on to (A) and (B). Strong tendency to (C). Cu clouds over (A) and (B)	Slack tendency on shores (A) and (B). Continuing tendency to (C). Cu clouds begin to disperse. Katabatic descent starts on (A). Anabatic ascent may continue on (B)	Katabatic drift from (A) and slack tendency on (B) lead to wind from (A) to (B). However, add continuing tendency to (C)
South	Anabatic drift up (B). Developing tendency for drift up (A). Slack tendency towards (C). Cu clouds mainly over (B)	Equal tendencies to anabatics on to (A) and (B) Some tendency to (C) but not as marked as when (C) looks north. Cu clouds over (A) and (B)	Slack tendency on shores (A) and (B). Slight tendency to (C). However, generally slackening thermal tendencies at this end of lake. Main tendency is N flow along lake. Katabatic descent starts on (B) when shadowed	Katabatic drift from (B) and starting katabatic on (A) Wind tends to be from (B) to (A). Little tendency to (C)
East	Anabatic drift up both (A) and (B) but (A) preferred. Little tendency towards (C) at first, but developing	Anabatic drift mainly to shore (A) so wind (B) to (A). Strong tendency to (C) so add E drift	Slackening tendency to anabatics on (A) and (B). Katabatics may start on (B). Flow to (C) continues and so main wind is E drift	Katabatics from (B) and (A). Flow to (C) slackens. Strong tendency to calm

The tendencies are those of an otherwise calm situation. Nights with clear skies will have these tendencies even when there are moderate daytime winds. However, by day topographic cants and thermal tendencies can be over-ridden by the gradient wind.

Early night	Middle of the night	Early hours	Sunrise	Gradient wind from:
Strong katabatic descent from both (A) and (B). Hug shores for wind, avoid calm centre. Tendency for backbone of Cu cloud to develop along centre-line of lake. Slack flow in (C)	Katabatics continue from (A) and (B) as for early night. Developing flow down (C), so N flow along lake	Flow from (C) dominant as katabatics from (A) and (B) slacken to nothing	Continuing flow from (C) but diminishing as sun climbs. Slack anabatic tendency on (A) and (B) but developing on (A) as sun climbs	SW to SE—lake wind from S. NW to NE—lake wind from N. W or E—consider the holes through which the wind can find its way on to the lake surface
Strong katabatic descent from both (A) and (B). Hug shores for wind. Avoid calm centre. Tendency for backbone of Cu cloud to develop along lake centre and so show that this wind regime is in being	Katabatics continue as for early night. Developing flow down (C), so S flow along lake	Flow from (C) dominant as katabatics from (A) and (B) slacken to nothing. Thus S wind along lake	Continuing flow from (C) but diminishing as sun climbs. Slack anabatic tendency on (A) and (B) at first but developing on (B) as sun climbs	As above
Slack flow in (C). Strong katabatic descent from both (A) and (B). Katabatics also in (C) but little tendency to flow along (C). Cloud backbone possible as above	Katabatic flow from (A) and (B) and developing tendency for flow from (C)	Katabatics tend to diminish but flow from (C) continues. Thus any wind is drift from E to W. Loses vigour nearer centre of lake	Continuing flow from (C) to which must be added increasing tendency to anabatics up sunlit slopes	SW to NW—lake wind from W. NE to SE—lake wind from E. N or S—consider holes through which the wind can come to lake surface

111

(Contd. over)

Valley C looks	Morning regime	Early afternoon	Late afternoon	Evening
West	Anabatic drift up both (A) and (B) but (B) preferred. Slack tendency up (C) at first but rapidly developing	Anabatic drift overwhelmingly to shore (B). Strong tendency to flow to (C)	Anabatics continue on (B) but slack, or katabatics commence on (A). Flow to (C) continues	Katabatics commence on both (A) and (B) and flow to (C) slackens. Strong tendency to calm

Note: When lakes point between N–S and E–W directions or there are other situations not apparently covered, use the principle that sunlit slopes develop onshore drift and lately shaded ones develop offshore drift.

When gradient wind tends to over-ride thermal tendencies then consider other possibilities. Examples include:

1. Developing Cu which deepen with the morning. Showers or perhaps thunderstorms (falling winds). Look for direction of motion of lowest cloud as indicating true gradient wind and assume later falling winds come from that direction preferentially.

2. Increasing veil of high cloud with mare's tails and later halo phenomena. Gradient wind will normally back and increase. Rain belt likely to follow.

Early night	Middle of the night	Early hours	Sunrise	Gradient wind from:
Strong katabatic descent from both (A) and (B). Katabatics also in (C) but little tendency to flow along valley floor on to lake. Cloud backbone as above	Flow from (C) develops and adds to continuing katabatic flow from (A) and (B)	Katabatics tend to diminish but flow from (C) continues. Thus gentle breeze along lake is possible. However, allow for it losing vigour farther from the head of the lake	Continuing flow from (C) but increasing tendency to anabatics up sunlit slopes	As above

3. Continuous moderate rain now. After requisite time interval (1–6 hours) gradient wind should veer with cessation of rain.
4. Warm, cloudy airstream—usually from between S and W—must be followed by veer and cold front which only forecast can usually predict.
5. Belt of heavy showers now. Expect veer and clearance followed by more showers by day.
6. Hot sultry conditions with passing belts of Ac (plus other clouds). Expect thunderstorms from same direction as Ac comes. Allow for arriving over slopes without much warning and producing up to gale force downdraught (falling winds).
7. On European lakes allow for föhn conditions (also elsewhere when mountain range lies in gradient wind direction) i.e. unnatural clarity of the air and stillness followed by sudden arrival of wind from mountains up to gale force, especially when funnelled through valley constrictions.

As well as the winds which are forecast there will be some special winds on large lakes. These will be the dominant winds when there is already very little gradient wind in the morning. The lakes version of the sea breeze is the lake breeze that can vary the wind over the shoreline on almost any summer day. It gets 8 miles inland on 3–4 days of a typical late spring or summer month. If the forecast or actual morning wind is less than 5–8 kt mean speed then consider a lake breeze.

Will there be a Lake Breeze?

Remarks apply to shores with an uninterrupted and more or less straight shoreline backed by an extensive, flattish hinterland. E and S facing shores will be preferred to W facing. N facing shores have least chance of lake breeze.

(The information refers to the Great Lakes of North America but should, with reservations, be applicable to other large bodies of inland water.)

Best weather type	Look of the day	Morning wind from shorewards	Other morning wind directions
High centred over area. Weather chart should otherwise show vary widely spaced isobars. Forecast should not go for rapid movement of the High	Sunny early and no more than half cover of cloud by midday. Light or gentle wind. Near calm in early morning	Same as sea breeze frontal system but less deeply penetrating. However, same early calms over shoreside waters, then breeze arrives at places inland progressively later, i.e. 1030 LST 1–2 miles inland. 1330–1630 LST at 8–10 miles inland. (Refers to E facing shore. System weaker when W facing)	Parallel to shore or slightly on-shore. If fully on-shore then lake breeze only adds to existing wind

What is the Wind speed over the Lake?

1. Obtain a reliable wind speed over land.
2. Use time of day in table below to find factor by which to multiply wind speed over land to give speed over water.

Spring and early summer (mid February–June)

LST	01	03	06	08	10	12	14	16	18	20	22	24
Factor	2·5	2·4	2·2	1·9	1·4	1·1	1·0	1·1	1·2	1·9	2·3	2·5

Summer and fall/autumn (July–November)

LST	01	03	06	08	10	12	14	16	18	20	22	24
Factor	2·8	2·7	2·5	2·2	1·8	1·3	1·2	1·4	1·9	2·5	2·6	2·8

What is the Lake Breeze Season?

On average, breezes are first possible at the beginning of April, when lake breeze occurs only with almost total calm. The season is generally from mid April to mid August. Maximum effect is to be expected in June and July. Very little chance of lake breeze from September through to March.

What is the likely direction over the Lake? Given the wind direction ashore, expect the wind to veer (shift clockwise) on average 30–40° over the lake.

Most likely type of onset near shoreline	Evening and night	Weather type that inhibits breezes
Facing the lake: If wind along the coast from left expect: rapid or even sudden shift when lake breeze starts up. If from the right expect: slow shift to lake breeze direction. With winds of about 6–8 kt mean speed a partial shift to more on-shore, but no true on-shore lake breeze as with lighter winds If wind truly off-shore expect: Sea breeze frontal system with calming near shore at first then onset and gradual strengthening with the afternoon. If wind truly on-shore expect: Reinforced speed by afternoon and perhaps some shift to more directly on-shore	Expect to go calm in evening if forecast not for rapid movement of prevailing pressure pattern. Expect some nocturnal wind overnight with light wind from land guided by shore topography. Stronger where mountains come close to lake edge, i.e. moderate katabatics sometimes. Expect faltering of nocturnal wind near dawn	Cyclonic isobars with only occasional glimpses of the sun. Even when sunny not so likely as with anticyclonic. However, lows may move out during day to give a chance of a late breeze, if wind light and there is sunshine and reasonable visibility

HAVE YOU CONSIDERED?

Hints on pre-race planning and advice on easy day sailing.
You may not wish or be able to answer all these real or implied questions—they are simply designed to prompt.

Race Planning Restricted waters.
Things to establish before the race

Likely gradient wind direction can be found from	Likely type of airstream	Proximity of topography	Possible local shifts	Tidal streams etc
1. Forecaster at a local weather station 2. Telephone pre-recorded forecast 3. Telephone fax actual and forecast charts 4. TV forecast that also gives current charts 5. Radio forecast for inshore and offshore	1. Unstable: Likely strength? Strength of gusts? Showers? Thunderstorms? 2. Stable: Strength? When will inversion break? Morning or afternoon? Any fog?	Local contour map Cliffs Promontories Valleys Islands (most important when airstream stable) Bays	Shoreside shifts Gusts over cliffs Bending over islands and promotories Sea breezes (stable) bent when coming up against high ground. Flow into bays. Holes in the wind in lee of islands	State of tide during race Set of streams past marks and coastal inlets Streams emptying from estuaries Back eddies in bays

Things to establish on the spot

Mean wind direction	Mean wind mark	Type of airstream	Position of marks and wind direction	Sea breeze?
See (16)	Try to establish a sight mark in the eye of the mean wind as far away as possible. Use as a reference for shifts.	Cu day (74) or (90). Warm, poor visibility day (84) or (100). Showery day (80) or (96) can be expected	Inshore marks: Shoreside shifts? Sea breeze shifts? Offshore marks Sea breeze shifts or calms? (46)	Possible? (52) When? (53)

Things that help the day go smoothly

Know the way the wind blows	Ensure the wind later will not be uncomfortable	Look for possible trouble	Quiet mornings
Get the forecast the night before and in the morning. Methods are given above.	If leaving shelter use (17) and add gusts (19). Too much seaway? (20)	Forecasts can be wrong. If sky and wind conspire against you (30) and (34) should you come home now?	Often mean quieter evenings. Will tide be running out against you, making a long haul home? Also mean sea breezes in middle of day and sea breeze calms in evening.

Photo 24 *(p. 115)*
Have you considered what a sky like this means? It is as well to be conversant with the look of the sky that foretells poor weather in the next six to ten hours. The weather is advancing through the picture. It is fair now, but the blue sky is crossed with vapour trails. Beyond that Ci and Cs whiten the upper sky; below darker clouds stream in. The regime, which it is rarely possible to capture in one photograph, spells impending trouble.

Fronts etc.	*If frontal shifts?*	*If sea breeze shift?*	*If very late finish*
Any fronts likely to cross area? (30). Shifting pressure systems? Lows (24)	New wind veered to old and new wind quality (30) and (64)	Most likely new direction is 10–20° left of directly onshore. Consider other lesser shifts in moderate winds	Lose sea breeze? Shift back to gradient replacing sea breeze? Flat calm? Don't forget the paddle! And an anchor? With enough line to reach the bottom

When sea breeze blows	*Review large scale shift timing*	*Quality assessment*	*Leaving shelter?*
What is new tactical situation?	Cannot time fronts accurately enough, so eye to windward if frontal situation (photo 24) passing. Is warm front coming (30)?	Recognize normal shift day (74) or (90) and time shift pattern. Recognize abnormal shift pattern if it exists and time shift pattern. Assume tacking to variables paramount and other tactical considerations secondary	Hot ashore but cool or cold on water (Maine coast e.g.). Therefore protective clothing plus personal buoyancy. Any risk of thunderstorms? With possible gusts and cold deluge. Lesser situations equally important, so take precautions

The tide	*The river*	*If you must go back early*
Don't let it leave you stranded up the creek. If you are not familiar with a drying tidal area, leave it 2 hours after high water. Is there a bar (not for thirst but across the harbour entrance)? Ebb tide race in the entrance?	Go upstream if you have a choice—drift home	Sail in the morning as there will be wind by lunchtime and in the afternoon. Get back by 1700 LST. Thus escape evening calm

Other Books

Other books by the author that help amplify and explain the reasons for statements made in the tables of this book.

Instant Weather Forecasting (Adlard Coles Nautical, Sheridan House Inc). The bestselling do-it-yourself weather forecast book which has been continuously in print since 1967, has been translated into a dozen languages and is now reissued in an updated Second Edition. It forms a companion to this volume.

Reading the Weather: Modern Techniques for Yachtsmen (Adlard Coles Nautical). A highly illustrated book for yachtsmen who wishes to understand and predict his own weather based on the information now available through modern technology. (Now out of print.)

The Weather Handbook (Waterline, Sheridan House Inc). An up to date explanatory book for all those interested in the weather. Highly illustrated throughout.

Wind and Sailing Boats (David and Charles). The author's 'right-now' weather book for small craft sailors. (Now out of print.)